Implementing Activity-Based Management in Daily Operations

John A. Miller

NAM/Wiley Series in Manufacturing

John Wiley & Sons; Inc.
New York • Chichester • Brisbane • Toronto • Singapore

Library of Congress Cataloging-in-Publication Data:
Miller, John A., 1948–
    Implementing Activity-Based Management in Daily Operations
John A. Miller.
        p.   cm.
    Includes index.
    ISBN 0-471-04003-7 (alk. paper)
    1. Activity-based costing.   2. Cost accounting.   3. Managerial
accounting.
    HF5686.C8M523   1996
    658.15'11—dc20   95-20153
                                                                    CIP

Printed in the United States of America

10 9 8 7 6 5 4 3

Dedication and Acknowledgments

I am reminded of a holiday weekend in 1987, when my good friend Alan Rush and I worked through a three-day weekend to prepare a training seminar for the American Productivity & Quality Center, titled *Implementing Activity-Based Cost Management*. I was interested in the new cost-tracing methodologies and how these techniques could be used to provide more accurate costs of products and services, and I wanted to focus the training material on activity-based costing. In his infinite wisdom, Alan insisted that the real value of these new techniques was in their role of initiating, supporting, driving, and measuring process improvement initiatives and in improved decision making. It was activity management that was important and needed to be emphasized. It was more than activity-based costing: It was activity-based management. That weekend I learned from Alan, yet he never sent me a bill. As payment, all he asked was that I learn everything I could about ABM/ABC and to share the knowledge with others. For that reason, I have dedicated this book to Alan.

This is a book about what I have learned since that weekend. Every business opportunity since then has given me a chance to work with others as a way to explore and learn these new management techniques. I am indebted to Jim Brimson, John Campi, George Foster, Bill Hubbell, Larry Maisel, Terry Newlin, Chris Pieper, Tom Pryor, Mike Roberts, and Dan Swenson for all that I have learned by working with them. I am thankful for what I have learned from the individuals and associations I worked with on a regular basis. Organizations like the APQC, CAM-I, SEMATECH, INCAE University, and the International Benchmarking Clearinghouse. Individuals like John Antos, Fred Barnes, Richard Brown, Jack Grayson, Robert Mendoza, Carla O'Dell, Jim Schmook, Carl Thor, Ashok Vadgama, and Pete Zampino. Perhaps the most important learning took place in the client offices, where the principles, theories, and philosophies of ABM were applied and tested. Hundreds of names come to mind. I wish I could name you individually. Thank you so much.

I am also grateful to Arthur Andersen and the role they have played in my career and development. After a 15 year absence (I joined in 1970 and spent the first eight years of my career with them), I rejoined Arthur Andersen as a Principal with the Cost Management Competency Center to assist companies worldwide to realize measurable performance improvement and positive, lasting change. While much has changed in the last 25 years, the basic values of client service, employee development and leadership displayed then remain the same today. I wish to thank Arthur Andersen thought leaders including Steve Hronec, Chuck Ketteman, Chuck Marx, and Steve Player.

As any author will attest, there are always special thanks owed to those people that provided encouragement and support. These special thanks go to Sheila Busby, Joe and Jude Compofelice, and Barbara Price. Finally, I am grateful for the sacrifices made by my wife and family: Kathy, Lisa, and Michael. These sacrifices enabled me to spend the time required to write this book.

John Miller
December 4, 1996

Contents

10 Ongoing System Requirements   175

11 Full Integration   193

The CAM-I Glossary of Activity-Based Management   209

Preface

In its June 6, 1988 issue, *Business Week* magazine published a special report titled, "The Productivity Paradox." This special report noted that the United States lagged behind other industrial countries in productivity growth. The problem was defined by *Business Week:* "We focused on capital investment as a way to reduce labor—ignoring the huge benefits to be gained from improved quality, reduced inventories, and faster introduction of new products. We need a new math for productivity."

In its article *"How the New Math of Productivity Adds Up,"* *Business Week* pointed out that "The principles of current cost management systems were laid down soon after the Securities Exchange Act of 1934, in an era when labor was the chief variable cost, when mass production and the tenets of efficiency expert Fredrick W. Taylor propelled U.S. industry to world dominance."

In this article, *Business Week* drew heavily on the work of Texas-based Consortium for Advanced Manufacturing-International (CAM-I), which had been founded to develop software standards for the world's advanced factories. Through its cost management task force composed of three dozen large U.S. and European manufacturers, the Big Six accounting firms, the Pentagon, and the Institute of Management Accountants, "new rules for cost management as investment justification, product costing, the total life-cycle costs of products, and how to define better measures of manufacturing performance" were developed. These new approaches were often radically different from traditional techniques. These new approaches were generally referred to as activity-based costing (ABC).

Since CAM-I published its initial work in 1989 (*Cost Management in Today's Advancement Manufacturing Environment*), the use and application of ABC has continued to evolve. No longer is its applicability limited to manufacturing organizations. The principals and philosophies of activity-based thinking apply equally to service companies, government agencies, and process industries. The acronym itself has evolved from ABC to ABCM (activity-based cost management) to ABM (activity-based management), as the application of ABC evolved from a manufacturing product costing orientation to a management philosophy of activity management applied in industries and organizations other than manufacturing.

Since its initial publications, CAM-I has become the recognized standard for ABM guidelines and definitions. This book draws heavily on the work of CAM-I. All definitions used in this book are based on Version 1.2 of the CAM-I *Glossary of Activity Based Management,* which is reproduced in its entirety and included in the appendix. When a term from the CAM-I glossary is first defined in this book, it will appear in italic print, together with its definition. Clarification and interpretation will be provided by the author.

This is a book for all members of an organization interested in implementing ABM. It is not intended for only cost accounting and finance managers. Accordingly, examples and illustrations have been simplified to explain and demonstrate the principles, philosophies, and application of ABM. Some of the more technical aspects of ABM, like the development of ABM product cost standards, the consideration of accounting for and tracing excess capacity costs, and the considerations for determining and tracing fully depreciated assets, will not be covered. Cost accounting and finance managers must seek additional sources of information to meet the specific technical areas they may encounter when implementing ABM.

1

Introduction

Management practices and methods have changed over the last decade and will continue to change beyond the year 2000. Organizations are moving from managing vertically to managing horizontally. It is a move from a functional orientation to a process orientation. Total quality management (TQM), just-in-time (J-I-T), benchmarking, and business process reengineering (BPR) are all examples of horizontal management improvement initiatives. These initiatives are designed to improve an organization's work processes and activities to effectively and efficiently meet or exceed changing customer requirements. Management information systems to track and provide information about the horizontal aspects of a business have lagged significantly behind the needs of its managers.

Activity-based costing/activity-based management (ABC/ABM) fills this information need by providing cost and operating information that mirrors the horizontal view. The focus of ABC is on accurate information about the true cost of products, services, processes, activities, distribution channels, customer segments, contracts, and projects. Activity-based management makes this cost and operating information useful by providing value analysis, cost drivers, and performance measures to initiate, drive, or support improvement efforts and to improve decision making.

1

ACTIVITIES AS COMMON DENOMINATOR

Activities are the common denominator of the horizontal organization. This can be demonstrated through a simple model that illustrates the horizontal, or process-based, view of an organization (see Exhibit 1–1). This model applies to all organizations, including manufacturing companies, service companies, schools, universities, federal and state government agencies, and even fraternal organizations.

Placed at the top of the process-based organization are the needs and requirements of customers. Every organization exists to meet these needs and requirements. If there is no customer need, there is no need for the organization. To varying degrees, every organization has processes and activities in place to convert capital, materials, and purchased services to products/services required by their customers. This is represented in the middle of the model. Processes and activities represent the value added by the organization. Placed at the bottom of the model are the measures of organizational performance. Performance measures for vendors, suppli-

Exhibit 1–1.   Process-Based Organization

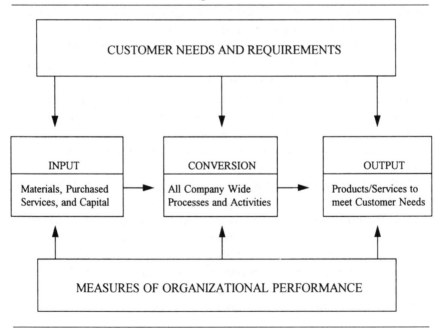

ers, customer service, processes, products, services, and activities are necessary to make judgments on how well the organization is performing. Financial measures of performance indicate whether the organization is performing at the level necessary to satisfy its stockholders.

Processes and activities are the central nervous system of the process-based organization and represent the core of what the organization does to create value for its customers and stockholders. Competition is based on the performance of products and services in the marketplace and driven by the performance of the processes and activities used to create, make, and deliver them. In essence, competitors compete at the activity and process level. Products and services represent the output of the organization's processes and activities.

Many organizations find that, when compared to competitors, each has access to the same raw materials, capital, technology, equipment and machinery, vendors and suppliers, labor pools, and customers. Competitors in these situations differentiate themselves mostly on the basis of activity and process performance, because activity performance may be the only source of competitive advantage. Even companies that dominate markets must continue to improve activities if they intend to remain dominant over the long term.

Performance of activities is the cornerstone and common denominator of improvement initiatives. Managers and employees of all organizations are constantly focused with improving their processes and activities to remain competitive. Regardless of the improvement methodology used, each has the same objective; to improve processes and activities. Those organizations that execute their processes and activities with the highest level of quality, the least amount of cycle time, and the lowest amount of cost are those most likely to win in the end.

Most organizations today have formal improvement initiatives in place. Known generically as TQM, J-I-T, or BPR, or given specific names like Quality is Job1 (Ford Motor Company), these management improvement initiatives all share a philosophy of continuous improvement. The Consortium for Advanced Manufacturing-International (CAM-I) defines *continuous improvement* as a program to eliminate waste, reduce response time, simplify the design of both products and processes, and improve quality.

Many organizations position their continuous improvement initiatives as something new. It is not unusual for a company to indicate that they started continuous improvement efforts within the last year, the last two years, or the last five years. Often they point to a specific date or period of time when continuous improvement efforts were initiated, as if to say improvements were not taking place before then. However, most managers have been trying to improve the operations and activities of their organizations since the day they started working.

There are many differences in continuous improvement today, versus how it might have been viewed five or ten years ago. One difference is the orientation toward process improvement as opposed to problem solving. Improvement in days past came from solving problems and putting out fires. Today, however, organizations focus on improving activities and processes to prevent problems. Also different is empowerment and the willingness to push responsibility for improvement further down the organization. Historically, people brought problems to managers for solution. Continuous improvement today involves empowering people to improve processes. Another difference is the return of the external customer to prominence. Historical improvement efforts tended to focus on internal problems. Now focus is on empowering people to improve processes that serve an external customer requirement. Finally, the level of competition and the intensity of improvement requirements has been elevated. In days long past, it was acceptable for organizations to improve productivity 2 or 3% per year and still remain competitive. Today, with increased global competition, many companies and industries find that unless they improve productivity 10, 15, or even 20% per year, they are destined for failure. It is a more competitive world today, and the stakes are raised.

Management must focus on the process/horizontal view of their organizations to remain competitive. Activities represent the horizontal view. Activity-based management is a tool developed to support the process-based organization by providing information and data needed to plan, manage, control, and direct the activities of a business to improve processes, products, and services, to eliminate waste, and to execute business operations and strategies. This information takes the form of the outputs of an ABM information system.

OUTPUTS OF ACTIVITY-BASED MANAGEMENT INFORMATION SYSTEM

Organizations that are designing and implementing ABM will find there are five basic information outputs for the new system. These include the following:

1. The cost of activities and business processes.
2. The cost of non-value-added activities.
3. Activity-based performance measures.
4. Accurate product/service cost (cost objects).
5. Cost drivers.

These information outputs are discussed in the following.

The Cost of Activities and Business Processes

Since activities form the very core of what a business does, the basic output of the ABM system must be to provide relevant cost information about each significant activity. Cost information about what the business does (i.e., about its activities) is a fundamental information output of the new system.

As defined by CAM-I, an *activity* is (1) work performed within an organization and (2) the aggregations of actions performed within an organization that are useful for purposes of ABC. Activities are work processes performed in an organization. They are, in essence, aggregations of tasks (whether performed by people or machines) required to satisfy the needs of customers (whether internal or external). *Processes* are a series of activities that are linked to perform a specific objective. For example, the assembly of a television set or the paying of a bill or claim entails several linked activities.

Viewing an organization from the perspective of activity cost can be enlightening . . . or frightening. Traditionally, organizations report cost on a functional basis (departments or sections) and by expense type (salaries, supplies, travel, etc.). Traditional systems report what money is spent for and by whom but fail to report the cost of activities and processes. A simple illustration of the process-based view of cost, as compared with traditional cost viewpoints, is displayed in Exhibit 1–2. As illustrated in this Exhibit, the total annual cost of Joe's cake shop is $700,000 and is viewed from the perspective of department cost, expense types, and activities. From each viewpoint, the total cost of the business is the same. It is just a different way of looking at the same total cost structure. Most organizations do not report the process or activity view of cost. Activity-based management information systems are designed to report business process and activity cost.

Exhibit 1–2. Process-Based View of Cost

Joe's Cake Shop

Departments		Expense Types		Processes/Activities	
Sales	$50,000	Salaries	$400,000	Take Orders	$70,000
Production	350,000	Materials	125,000	Make Cakes	
Transportation	100,000	Supplies	25,000	Mix Batter	250,000
General and		Depreciation	88,000	Bake Layers	150,000
Administrative	200,000	Rent	62,000	Frost Cake	90,000
				Deliver Cakes	140,000
Total	$700,000	Total	$700,000	Total	$700,000

The Cost of Non-Value-Added Activities

Some activities add value to a product or service, while some do not. A *non-value-added activity* is an activity that is considered not to contribute to customer value or to the organization's needs. The designation non-value added reflects a belief that the activity can be redesigned, reduced, or eliminated without reducing the quantity, responsiveness, or quality of the output required by the customer or the organization.

The definition of a *value-added activity* is the same as that of a non-value-added activity, stated in the positive: An activity that is judged to contribute to customer value or satisfy an organizational need. The attribute value added reflects a belief that the activity cannot be eliminated without reducing the quantity, responsiveness, or quality of output required by a customer or organization.

In a manufacturing operation, the cost and time associated with activities of moving parts, rework, and setup are often cited examples of non-valued-added activities. These non-value-added activities represent *waste,* defined as resources consumed by unessential or inefficient activities. Waste is not limited to factory floor or production operations. Many non-factory/production activities include rework, inefficiency, redundancy, and duplication. Virtually every organization will acknowledge the existence of work that could be done more efficiently or should never have been done at all.

Identification of the cost of non-value-added activities has enormous value to management. This crucial information output provides a focal point for improvement efforts designed to eliminate non-value-added work and waste as much as possible. In addition, every value-added activity includes non-value-added tasks. Activity cost and performance, when linked to the task level, provides information useful to improving a value-added activity. Non-value-added tasks like rework loops, corrections, or duplicated efforts can be quantified and targeted for reduction, thus improving the value-added activity.

Activity-Based Performance Measures

In addition to cost information for business processes and activities, the ABM system must report information and data on activity performance. Knowing the total cost of an activity is insufficient to measure activity performance. Activity measures of quality, cycle time, productivity, and customer service may also be required to judge activity performance.

Performance measures and measurement is a broad topic and covers many aspects of a business, as illustrated by definition. *Performance measures* are defined as indicators of the work performed and the results achieved in an activity, process, or organizational unit. Performance measures may be financial or nonfinancial. An example of a performance measure of an activity is the number of defective parts per million. An example of a performance measure of an organization unit is return on sales.

Activity-based management systems focus on measuring the performance of activities and processes by assessing the quality, cycle time, productivity, and customer satisfaction elements of activity performance. Each of these information elements has limited value when viewed independently because in isolation none of them can fully measure performance or fully describe how well the organizational activities are being performed. For example, productivity improvements would not be meaningful if cycle times were increasing or customer service levels declining. Each of these activity performance measurements must be considered in tandem when judging total activity performance.

Measuring the performance of activities provides a scorecard to report how well improvement efforts are working and is an integral part of continuous improvement. Therefore, a key output of an ABM system is the measurement of performance at the activity and business process level.

Accurate Product/Service Cost (Cost Objects)

Products and services are provided to markets and customers through various distribution channels or contractual relationships. Because products and services consume resources at different rates and require different levels of support, costs must be accurately determined. Accurate product and service cost information is vital for selecting the individual and segmented markets where an organization competes and for pricing in those markets. Accurate product and service cost information is a key information output of the ABM system.

True product or service cost is the summation of all resources consumed in creating, producing, designing, supporting, and delivering a product or service to a customer. Activity-based product/service cost information encompasses cost beyond the factory floor, to identify the total cost (i.e., including distribution and support costs) associated with a product or service. Product/service cost can be driven down for a particular market, customer, or distribution channel. Activity-based management systems provide accurate cost information by linking the consumption of activities directly to products or services that require the activity.

In the ABC world, products and services are referred to as *cost objects,* defined as any customer, product, service, contract, project, or other work unit for which a separate cost measurement is desired. The term cost object is used because the principles and methods of ABC have application beyond product and service cost. These methods are equally useful in determining the true cost of projects, contracts, programs, distribution channels, or customer segments.

While product/service cost has strategic value, its operational value is limited to directing managers to products or services that consume too many resources to be competitive in a particular market, product, or customer group. Operational improvements can only come from improving the processes and activities used to design, produce, and deliver the product or service to the customer.

Cost Drivers

The final output of an ABM system is cost driver information. *Cost driver* is any factor that causes a change in the cost of an activity. For example, the quality of parts received by an activity (e.g., the percent that are defective) is a determining factor in the work required by that activity, because the quality of parts received affects the resources required to perform the activity. An activity may have multiple cost drivers associated with it.

Practice would dictate a slight change in the CAM-I definition: from an activity *may* have multiple cost drivers associated with it, to an activity *will* have multiple cost drivers associated with it. A cost driver is any factor that causes a change in the total cost of an activity. It is, in short, the cause of cost, and there are many of them. Understanding the causal relationship between an activity and its cost enables management to focus improvement efforts on those areas that will produce the best results.

For example, a business process for a company that provides a service to manufacturers by collecting and processing product and demographic information about customers includes an activity of entering the raw data into a database. Customers provide this information in the form of a warranty card. Productivity in this company is measured as a cost per card or the cost to enter a customer response.

Improvement efforts focused on making data entry clerks (the company's major cost) work harder and faster produced mixed results. As part of its ABM initiative, the company instituted a cost driver analysis. This analysis discovered that, more than any other factor, the design of the warranty card was the root of cost in data entry. Poorly designed cards that were difficult to read slowed the data entry operators. Armed with this information, management focused its improvement efforts on the card design activity and ultimately achieved performance improvements in the data entry activity.

As this example shows, by identifying and reporting cost drivers this information directed management toward areas where improvement efforts produced the best result. When cost drivers are quantifiable (e.g., number of parts causal to manufacturing overhead or number of feet traveled causal to factory logistics cost), improvement efforts that focus on reducing the number of parts or decreasing the distance traveled can be measured.

In summary, the ABM outputs described earlier—the cost of activities and business processes, the cost of non-value-added activities, measures of activity performance, accurate product/service cost (cost objects), and cost drivers—all contribute to management improvement initiatives and improved decision making by providing cost and operating information about the activities of the organization.

HISTORY OF ACTIVITY-BASED MANAGEMENT

The recent roots of ABM can be traced to Texas-based CAM-I through its cost management system (CMS) project task force. Founded in 1972, CAM-I is a nonprofit consortium of advanced manufacturers. The original purpose of CAM-I was to study and establish systems, methods, equipment standards, and computer platforms so that manufacturing machines and equipment could communicate with each other in the factory of the future, the so-called "lights-out" factory, where no direct labor was performed by humans.

As part of their work, a secondary issue came up as it related to establishing the cost of products when there was no direct labor. Most of these CAM-I manufacturing companies calculated product cost by first identifying direct materials and direct labor consumed in production and then allocating overhead costs to products on the basis of direct labor. Specifically, the question was, How can product cost be calculated when there is no direct labor on which to allocate overhead? Hence, the CMS task force was established in 1986, led by financial people working for the advanced manufacturers of the consortium. The initial result of the CMS task force work was published in a book titled *Cost Management for Today's Advanced Manufacturers* (Berliner and Brimson 1988).

One of the main conclusions of the CMS task force was that products do not consume cost directly. Money is spent on activities, which in turn are consumed by products/services (cost objects). This new costing methodology and the two-stage allocation method (now known as ABC), made its first public appearance in articles published in the *Harvard Business Review* (Kaplan, Robert S., "One Cost System Isn't Enough," January–February, 1988, pp. 61–66 and Cooper, Robin and Kaplan, Robert S. "Measure Costs Right: Make the Right Decisions," September–October, 1988, pp. 96–103).

The difference between traditional allocation methods and the new activity-based tracing methods are illustrated in Exhibit 1–3. In this Exhibit, the traditional method of costing products and services is depicted as a solid line where the cost of overhead is allocated directly to products or services based on direct labor and direct material. The dotted line depicts the activity-based method where costs are first traced, or allocated, to activities (stage 1). Activity costs are then traced to products or services based on use (stage 2).

The roots of ABM lie in product costing. People did not begin to grasp the value of using activity information to support and drive improvement initiatives and understand its applicability to industries other than advanced manufacturing until the early 1990s. It was this understanding that led to the birth of ABM.

Exhibit 1–3. Two-Stage Tracing for Product/Service Costing

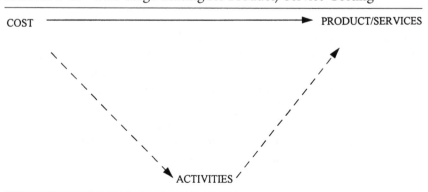

The similarities and differences between ABC and ABM can be expressed in their definitions:

> *Activity-based costing* is defined as a methodology that measures the cost and performance of activities, resources, and cost objects. Resources are assigned to activities, and then activities are assigned to cost objects based on their use.
>
> *Activity-based management* is defined as a discipline that focuses on the management of activities as the route to improving the value received by the customer and the profit achieved by providing this value. This discipline includes cost driver analysis, activity analysis, and performance measurement. Activity-based management draws on ABC as its major source of information.

In essence, ABC does the arithmetic to provide accurate cost information. Activity-based management is focused on using the information to manage activities. For a long time, ABM was viewed as applying only to manufacturing organizations in general and to advanced manufacturing specifically. That is because most of the initial activity-based implementations were done by members of the CAM-I consortium, all of which were advanced manufacturers and part of the original CMS task force. We know now that activities are universal to all organizations, including service companies, schools, governments, and not-for-profit organizations. In fact, ironically, most of the first ABC implementations were directed toward the service side of manufacturing—those overhead service activities that support product manufacturing.

BACK TO BASICS

In their book *Relevance Lost: The Rise and Fall of Management Accounting* (Boston: Harvard Business School Press, 1987), authors H. Thomas Johnson and Robert S. Kaplan successfully develop an argument that reporting cost and performance of activities is not new at all, only rediscovered. As far back as the 1850s, organizations were accounting and recording the cost of activities and the related activity outputs. Until the 1920s, managers invariably relied on information about the underlying processes, activities, transactions, and events that produced the financial numbers.

The requirement of audited financial statements and the development of generally accepted accounting principles (GAAP) for inventory costing and valuation purposes had a profound effect on management accounting. The focal point of the financial information produced by organizations became increasingly directed toward the external requirements of investors, banks, and regulatory agencies. Cost accounting became more important than cost management. By the 1960s and 1970s, managers commonly relied on the financial numbers alone, often ignoring the activities, transactions, and events that give rise to the financial numbers.

The pendulum has swung back. Like their nineteenth-century counterparts, managers again understand the importance of managing the underlying processes, activities, and transactions of the business. Financial numbers are the result and cannot be managed directly. Activities and processes, the common denominator of the horizontal organization, must be managed and improved to remain competitive. Activity management is fundamental and basic to organization success.

2

Uses and Benefits

Organizations implement ABM because they believe it will help them make better decisions, improve performance, and earn more money on assets deployed. Some managers will focus on performance measures as a way to effect behavior toward improvement. Others focus on reducing cost or increasing sales. Still for others, it is developing new products quickly. Many focus on process improvement. In some industries and for certain companies, improving performance requires personnel and other reductions when revenue and markets are in decline.

Regardless of philosophy or approach, each organization requires information to make decisions, set priorities, allocate resources, and monitor actions taken. Activity-based management systems exist only to meet this information requirement. The information and knowledge gained are of value and benefit only when people use the information to improve the business. This chapter will begin with the specific and general uses of activity-based information and will conclude with a review of its benefits.

SPECIFIC USES

Activity-based management information has wide use and applicability in the process-based organization. There are many uses of ABM informa-

tion. A ten-minute brainstorming session involving four ABM practitioners produced the following list of specific uses identified from completed
efforts:

- ◆ To determine product/service cost.
- ◆ To improve performance of processes and activities.
- ◆ To benchmark.
- ◆ To support improvement initiatives.
- ◆ To evaluate outsourcing of activities.
- ◆ To focus improvement efforts by identifying the "biggest bang for the buck."
- ◆ To drive a cultural change toward accountability and responsibility for the activities and processes of the business.
- ◆ To effect strategy deployment.
- ◆ To improve performance measurement system.
- ◆ To determine value-added/non-value-added activity costs and ratios.
- ◆ To cut cost/downsize.
- ◆ To budget.
- ◆ To determine and optimize activity capacity.
- ◆ To isolate/eliminate cost drivers.
- ◆ To charge intercompany cost for support services performed.
- ◆ To kick start dead total quality initiatives.
- ◆ To set target costs.
- ◆ To quantify the result of improvement initiatives.
- ◆ To estimate/bid on customer work.
- ◆ To manage projects and contracts.
- ◆ To consolidate operations.
- ◆ To evaluate acquisition candidates.

For purposes of review, this list can be consolidated into four main
areas. The most common area of use is to determine product/service
cost where accuracy is required for operational and strategic decisions of
product mix, product pricing, product line investments, and production
alternatives. A second common use is to support efforts directed toward

improving performance. A third common use is for organizations to use the information to reduce costs. The last area includes all other applications.

To Determine Product/Service Cost (Cost Objects)

Most ABM implementations to date have been directed toward product/service cost. Managers use ABC to determine the actual, true cost of products and services. The results are often astounding. Viewed from a true cost basis, organizations often find the following:

1. Traditional product/service cost systems calculate the cost of high-volume "standard" product/services at higher amounts than they really are. It would not be unusual to see misstatements of 5 to 15%. Conversely, low-volume "customized" product/service costs are stated at amounts less than true cost. These misstatements can be as high as 50%. These differences are the result of a *Cross-subsidy,* defined as the improper assignment of costs among cost objects such that certain cost objects are overcosted while other cost objects are undercosted relative to the activity costs assigned. For example, traditional cost accounting systems tend to overcost high-volume products and undercost low-volume products.

2. A relatively small percentage (30 to 40%) of product or service revenues can account for a large portion (60 to 70%) of profit.

3. When using the full potential of ABC, product/service costs (cost objects) can be calculated by distribution channel, customer segment, and/or geographical area. Activity based product/service cost can include distribution, sales, engineering, and even general and administrative costs. Organizations are often surprised to learn that many distribution channels, customer segments, and geographical areas are unprofitable when all activities associated with development, distribution, production, marketing, and sales are considered. It would not be unusual for an organization to learn that 60 to 70% of customers represent 100% of reported profits.

Organizations use ABC because they believe the understanding of true product/service cost will lead to better decisions of product mix, product pricing, and product sourcing. Better decisions lead to higher profits. However, knowing true product/service cost does not always result in better product/service decisions. If an organization is selling all it can at a market driven sales price, there may be no opportunity to increase selling price or change the mix of products. In these situations, accurate product/service cost information will force the organization to look at the activities associated with making or delivering an unprofitable product/service. To effect reductions in product/service cost, activities will have to be improved.

To Improve Performance of Processes and Activities

Many organizations use ABM as a structured way to select and examine those key activity work processes critical to the success of the organization. Activities are defined, analyzed, and costed to determine the "as is" situation. With the as is situation established, those activities/processes with high potential for improvement ("should be") can be selected and efforts/actions undertaken to realize the improvement opportunity. By identifying the biggest bang for the buck, improvement efforts can be focused.

Activity-based management information is also used to monitor the result of improvement initiatives. By reporting cost and performance of processes and activities, people and teams responsible for improvement have a scorecard to judge the result of effort. The ABM system is used to provide the feedback necessary to sustain improvement initiatives.

To Cut Cost/Downsize

Some organizations use ABM to cut cost, downsize, or restructure operations. This is the ugly side of ABM. But actually ABM is a very effective cost-cutting/reduction tool.

In situations where financial returns are unacceptable to stockholders or when survival is at stake, organizations often take significant cost reduction actions. These actions typically take the form of layoffs, plant closings, and idled equipment. Often taken across the board in all areas of the organization, they are rarely effective. Unless the volume of work is reduced, these cost reductions just leave the same work to be done by fewer people. Eventually, the cost creeps back into the organization.

Activity-based cost reduction is focused on the activities of the organization. Cut activities, cost will follow. In the words of Peter F. Drucker, notable author and management consultant, "The only truly effective way to cut costs is to cut out activities altogether. To try to cut back costs is rarely effective. There is little point in trying to do cheaply what should not be done at all."

Other Applications

With activities as common dominator of the process-based organization, it stands to reason that organizations can apply activity-based techniques and use activity-based information in a variety of ways. Organizations have applied the ABM tool to outsourcing evaluations, to bid customer work, to optimize activity capacity and for acquiring acquisition candidates. Several examples of other ABM applications are discussed below.

To evaluate outsourcing of activities

Many organizational activities can be subcontracted or sourced outside the organization. Managers constantly face a decision as to whether work should be done inside or outside the company. A decision to outsource is a decision to transfer the responsibility for activities to someone else, in turn for a fee. Managers often choose to outsource because it is cheaper. Someone else can perform activities in a more cost-effective way, while meeting the quality, cycle time, and service requirements of the activity.

An example of the use of ABM in an outsourcing application comes from a large organization based in Texas, which employs approximately 3,500 people. The manager of the payroll department in this organization was asked to evaluate a bid to outsource the payroll function to a service bureau specializing in payroll activities. As a basis for evaluation and recommendation, the payroll department manager undertook an activity-based evaluation of the payroll department. Activities were defined and costed, and the number of transactions (outputs) associated with the activities was determined. Once completed, this analysis was compared to the bid for services.

The evaluation produced interesting results. First, it was determined that many of the departmental activities would not go away with outsourcing. Activities associated with the collection, review, and correction of time attendance records remained with the company. Next, it was determined that the department was competitive, in terms of total dollars and by transaction, with those activities (preparing payroll checks, preparing payroll tax filings, maintaining payroll master file) included in the bid amount. The activity-based analysis enabled the manager to make an apples-to-apples comparison with the bid and to make a recommendation to keep the payroll function inside the company.

Despite the fact that the apples-to-apples comparison of internal costs was about the same as the bid amount, the manager took the position that the department was not competitive and needed to improve. That is because the manager knew the service bureau included a profit in the bid amount. Therefore, the estimated cost of performing the activities by the service bureau was less than the payroll department. Besides that, the analysis surprised the manager by highlighting the amount of money being spent on activities, like correcting errors, considered to be nonvalue added. With this knowledge, the manager took action to identify cost drivers and to focus efforts on improving the department activities.

To effect strategy deployment

Strategy is developed in the boardroom and deployed through processes and activities. In order to meet strategic goals, missions, and objectives, someone has to do something. Many organizations develop elaborate strategic plans then fail to determine that the necessary activities are in place to enable the plan to be accomplished. The likelihood of success in these situations is low.

The new director of strategic planning for a service company located in the midwest used ABM techniques as the basis for a strategic assessment prepared for the board of directors. Little progress had been made toward meeting strategic goals, and the board wanted to know why. The director performed a broad activity analysis to identify the ten most significant business processes and related activities currently being performed. Next, the director identified those business processes and activities required to meet strategic goals. The result of the analysis was to identify strategic activities that were underfunded or not done at all. This analysis clearly demonstrated that additional activities and activity capability were required to effectively deploy strategy.

To manage projects

A project is a series of activities, or steps, designed to meet a specific goal, objective, or outcome. Managing projects requires managing the activities required to complete the project. A regional CPA firm used ABM to strengthen its project management system. Projects were principally audits. Each audit project had a work program that consisted of the activities required to conduct an audit, such as testing compliance, confirming balances, observing physical inventories, and reviewing audit workpapers.

Individuals working on audit projects were required to record the actual hours worked on each audit activity performed. Project management was primarily focused on comparison of actual hours with the initial project estimates. Because auditors are compensated at varying rates based on experience, the CPA firm was interested in the cost of performing the audit activities as a way to strengthen its project management capability.

Not surprising to anyone who has ever worked on an audit, the activity of review audit workpapers consumed a significant portion of the total cost to conduct an audit. The result of this activity-based analysis indicated that it was more cost-effective to use higher-cost/experienced staff members to do certain audit activities because the cost of reviewing workpapers was lower.

To budget

Many managers budget by (1) taking current actual spending, (2) adding an inflation factor, and (3) including the wish list of items cut in the previous year budget negotiations. Department managers negotiate the budget amounts with their boss who in turn negotiate the budget amounts with additional bosses until agreement is met. These negotiations are usually centered around the amounts to be spent on salary, travel, supplies, and the other individual line items set forth in the budget. Rarely do these negotiations include discussions of the activities to be performed or level of activity performance expected.

Organizations that use ABM to budget typically start with defining the activity level necessary to support the expected sales volume or other requirements of the business. Once activity requirements have been agreed to, historical activity cost is used to establish an initial budget. Next, known or expected increases of labor or purchased services are then factored into the activity cost. Finally, planned cost reduction opportunities, less the cost of resources that may be required to implement the cost reduction opportunity, are reflected in the budget. The final budget thus includes the cost of activities the department has agreed to do, adjusted for inflation and quantified improvement targets.

To set target costs

Target costing is typically associated with product manufacturing companies and defined as a method used in the analysis of product and process design that involves estimating a target cost and designing the product to meet that cost. *Target cost* is defined as a cost calculated by subtracting a desired profit margin from an estimated (or a market-based) price to arrive at a desired production, engineering, or marketing cost. The target cost may not be the initial production cost, but instead the cost that is expected to be achieved during the mature production stage.

Introduced by the Japanese, target costing is a cost management tool. Used primarily to control manufacturing costs, target costing starts with the determination of the selling price a product must carry to capture a predetermined market share. Once the market driven product price is determined, the desired product profit is subtracted from the selling price to calculate the target product cost. Cost management is then directed toward improving the activities to design, produce, and distribute the product to the point required to meet the target. This is unlike many manufacturing organizations that calculate a product selling price by adding up direct material, labor, overhead, and a desired profit, with the hope that the resultant sales price is competitive in the marketplace.

The principles of activity-based target costing can be readily applied to nonmanufacturing companies. For example, a financially distressed mail order distributor of personal computer products operating under Chapter 11 of the U.S. Bankruptcy Code used target costing as the basis for a plan of reorganization to be submitted to principal creditors. A creditor-approved plan of reorganization is a prerequisite for emerging from bankruptcy.

In this application of target costing, selling price was estimated as total revenues less the cost of direct raw materials used to manufacture the product. Expected profit was the estimated payments creditors required as a condition for them to approve the plan. The difference was the target cost. The total cost of the company's activities had to fit inside the target cost box to have any chance of surviving and getting their plan of reorganization approved.

The company undertook an activity assessment to define, cost, and prioritize their business processes and activities. The objective of the assessment was to identify only those minimum activities necessary to operate the business under survival mode. All other activities and associated costs would be eliminated.

Because of the competitive situation in the industry and the company's position in its markets, management concluded that they were unable to structure the activities within the target cost box and elected to liquidate the business. Many businesses drag on through bankruptcy court for years, never emerging and slowly squandering the resources of the company. Creditors are left with nothing. In this example, management was able to use ABM techniques to look at the business objectively and make a decision based on the best interest of its creditors.

To determine and optimize activity capacity

Some businesses have sales and volume changes that vary widely over time. In these situations, managers need to determine and optimize capacity throughout the organization. Sometimes the swings in activity levels are seasonal in nature. Other times, changing activity levels float through the organization in peaks and valleys, creating excess capacity in some areas and under capacity in other areas.

The latter situation was true for a company involved in staging sporting events. Activity requirements varied widely as each event moved from initial planning to final accounting. Using ABM, the company identified the capacity of each key and significant activity performed. Activities were examined and analyzed to determine those that might be shared with other functions of the business as a way to optimize staff levels and to reduce the dependency on temporary personnel.

To estimate/bid on customer work

When electing to bid for customer work, the common practice is to include the cost of estimated materials, supplies, labor, overhead, and profit in the final submitted bid amount. In preparing the bid, estimates of the required materials, supplies, and labor are made. Overhead and support costs included in the bid amount are based upon an allocation of these costs. In using ABM information to prepare a bid/estimate for a customer, the activities required to meet the customer's requirements would be identified first. The bid amount would then be based, in part, on the cost of performing the activities.

The owner of a small company that performed clinical tests for organizations involved in the health care industry used ABM information as the basis of a new cost estimating system. First, activities associated with performing clinical tests, as well as activities associated with supporting the business, were identified and analyzed to determine the cost of performing individual activities. This information was documented in a database and linked to the new bid/estimating system. A new system was then developed where users specified activities required to meet the bid requirements. Final bids were based on materials, supplies, activity requirements, and profit expectations.

To consolidate operations

Activity-based information can be used to consolidate operations. Consolidating operations means putting activities and the people and equipment who perform them in one place. Operations are consolidated for many reasons. Most often, the reason is reduced work loads caused by, among other things, sales declines, changing technologies, and new entrants in competitive market places. Another reason is to make an organization more effective by putting similar functions and activities closer together. Because consolidating operations often means consolidating activities, it stands to reason that managers can make better decisions about consolidation when they have a complete understanding of the activities being consolidated.

To support acquisition analysis

One organization adopted ABM analysis and information as part of its acquisition strategy. Acquisition candidates were screened, in part, based on the strength of activities deemed to be critical to market success. Due diligence included an examination of those critical activities to determine activity cost, performance, and capacity. In addition, activities critical to meeting strategic and operating goals were identified and evaluated. This activity-based analysis enabled the acquisition team to drive their understanding of the acquisition candidate to a level sufficient to make better investment decisions.

It is interesting to note that the acquiring company focused on acquisitions where they believed activities were being performed at less than optimal levels. Their reasoning was simply that organizations that performed activities at an optimal level would tend to have higher profits and cash flow. In addition, organizations executing activities at a high level of performance might have little opportunity for improvement. Conversely, organizations performing activities poorly would tend to have lower profits and cash flow with more potential for improvement. Because the acquiring company based purchase price, in part, on cash flow, the purchase price of an organization performing activities at a high level of performance would be higher and have less opportunity for improvement.

To charge intercompany service costs

Organizations have used ABM information to establish the cost of services provided by one part of the organization to another part. For example, the data processing department of a large corporation had personal computer specialists who answered questions and provided support to users of personal computers. Activities and costs associated with these services were identified and used as the basis for internal service charges.

Users of these services were given the choice of using internal sources or going outside the organization. This enabled the users of services to make informed choices based on cost and service. In addition, by competing with the outside world, personal computer specialists were required to constantly improve service and reduce cost to remain competitive.

GENERAL USES

The specific applications and uses of ABM information previously discussed can be broadly divided into general categories that correspond to general situations. These general situations reflect the most frequent uses of ABM information by an organization given the specific operating environment and include the following:

1. Growing/expanding business.
2. No growth or flat.
3. Declining operations.
4. Capacity constrained.

These situations are illustrated in Exhibit 2–1.

Growth/Expanding Business

The first general situation is the growth/expanding business. In this situation, profit and productivity improve when sales increases are greater than cost increases. The focus is on eliminating/reducing non-value-added work so that resources can be redeployed to value-added activities. The objective is to avoid, or minimize, adding people and equipment. Managers focus on streamlining activities to squeeze out excess cost and waste for redeployment. Managers also need information to determine that activities important to future growth are adequately funded.

No Growth Business

The second general situation is the flat to no growth business. In this situation, profit and productivity increase by using fewer resources to maintain the same level of sales. Managers in these situations focus on the elimination/reduction of non-value-added work and the improvement of value-added work. Improving activity work processes by eliminating work

Exhibit 2–1. General Uses of Activity-Based Management Information

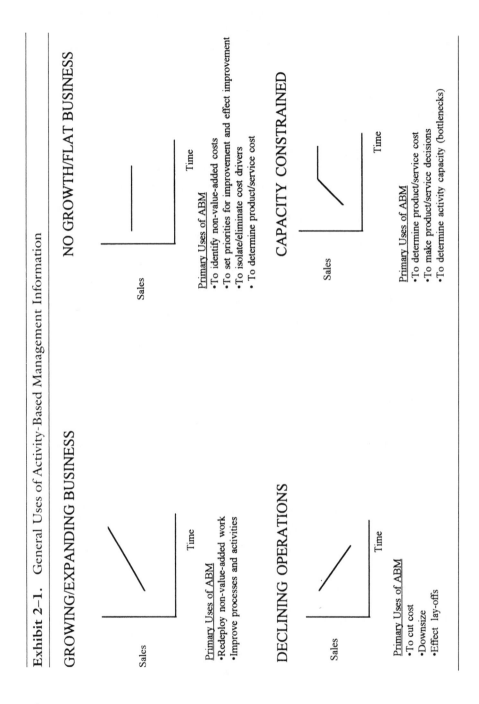

GROWING/EXPANDING BUSINESS

Sales

Time

Primary Uses of ABM
•Redeploy non-value-added work
•Improve processes and activities

NO GROWTH/FLAT BUSINESS

Sales

Time

Primary Uses of ABM
•To identify non-value-added costs
•To set priorities for improvement and effect improvement
•To isolate/eliminate cost drivers
• To determine product/service cost

DECLINING OPERATIONS

Sales

Time

Primary Uses of ABM
•To cut cost
•Downsize
•Effect lay-offs

CAPACITY CONSTRAINED

Sales

Time

Primary Uses of ABM
•To determine product/service cost
•To make product/service decisions
•To determine activity capacity (bottlenecks)

and absent resource reductions, results in additional capacity. Unless re-sources are eliminated or redeployed to areas where value can be created, there may be no improvement in the bottom line.

Organizations in this situation are faced with choices. Productivity and profitability can be increased in the short term by removing the additional capacity created by eliminating and improving work processes. That means layoffs or hiring freezes. Conversely, excess resources could be re-deployed to areas that would result in an expansion of sales or growth. In the no growth situation, most managers do not have the resources neces-sary to build their organizations. Resources are scarce and at the mainte-nance level. Eliminating and streamlining activity work processes create capacity and resources managers can use to build their organization.

Declining Operations

A third general situation is the rapidly declining business. In this situa-tion, sales declines typically mean there is less work to do, so activity ca-pacity and cost must be reduced just to stay even with sales reductions. As the business shrinks, activities must be consolidated and reduced. Man-agers faced with this situation use ABM information to get a fix on activ-ity capacity, to determine if the activity adds value to a changing market place, and to reduce cost. Managers that use ABM techniques in these sit-uations examine the organization's activities and make changes/reduc-tions based on the needs of customers and the strategic intent of the busi-ness. The result is intelligent cost cutting and reduction.

Capacity Constrained Business

Some industries and organizations are faced with the fortunate situation of demand exceeding the available capacity to produce a product or ser-vice. Managers faced with capacity constraints typically use ABM infor-mation for two reasons. The first reason is accurate product/service cost. Organizations are concerned that they may be selling products/services at a loss or minimum levels of profitability while turning profitable busi-ness away. When operating at capacity, product cost is critical for intelli-gent product mix decisions. The second reason is to determine activity capacity as a way to identify any activities that represent bottlenecks. Im-provement efforts can then be directed toward eliminating/reducing the bottlenecks to increase capacity.

BENEFITS OF IMPLEMENTATION

The value and benefit of ABM can only be measured by the decisions, actions, and improvements that result because people took, or were motivated to take, based on the knowledge and information provided. Implementors of ABM systems should be warned that all efforts to implement an ABM system will be wasted if no one uses or takes action on the information provided.

The benefits and value of an ABM system can be consolidated into three main areas known as the ABM value cycle, illustrated in Exhibit 2–2. These values and benefits are classified as process related, decision making, and performance measurements. Organizations can enter the value cycle at any point. As the ABM system matures, organizations migrate to multiple applications. This migration is important because a single use or application of activity-based information may not provide sufficient value to offset the cost of implementing and maintaining the system.

A prerequisite to benefiting from ABM is the willingness to assign responsibility for effecting those decisions, actions, and changes necessary to deliver the desired benefit. Decisions must be made, and actions must be taken. Specific responsibility has to be assigned to reduce/eliminate non-value-added activities, improve value-added activities, and reduce or eliminate the associated cost drivers.

Exhibit 2–2.   Activity-Based Management Value Cycle

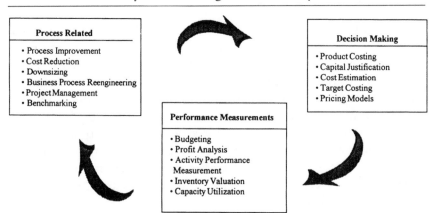

Process Related
• Process Improvement
• Cost Reduction
• Downsizing
• Business Process Reengineering
• Project Management
• Benchmarking

Decision Making
• Product Costing
• Capital Justification
• Cost Estimation
• Target Costing
• Pricing Models

Performance Measurements
• Budgeting
• Profit Analysis
• Activity Performance Measurement
• Inventory Valuation
• Capacity Utilization

The value and benefit of ABM can be difficult to quantify. The result of some decisions can be quantified, while others cannot. Expect people to want process improvements credited to their pet project or initiative. Supporters of TQM or BPR will argue that improvements are the result of these initiatives, even if driven by ABM information.

For example, an ABM analysis of processes and activities will identify those activities that have high potential for improvement, together with the associated cost drivers that cause this work to be done. An activity can be improved in many ways. A team assigned to reengineer a process/activity and to eliminate cost drivers would likely see their efforts as a BPR initiative. A team assigned to improve an activity may determine that the best way to effect improvement is to compare the activity with another company that performs that activity in a superior way. Rightfully so, this team would view their efforts as a benchmarking initiative.

Because ABM information drives and supports all improvement initiatives, regardless of acronym, it can be difficult to measure and quantify its role in improvement and decision making. Activity-based management measures the result of decisions and improvements, regardless of who or what initiative gets credit. While some organizations view ABM as a methodology for improvement, most do not. Most view it as a tool to support improvement initiatives and decision making. The dollar sign makes this information tool useful. Organizations and managers are bottom-line driven, and dollars and cents are the language of business. The dollar sign inspires people to action. The ABM information system tracks improvements and provides individuals, managers, and teams with process-based cost and operating information to judge the result of their decisions and efforts.

3

Overview of Implementation

Viewed from 40,000 feet.

A fully implemented ABM information system accumulates and reports activity-based information on a periodic basis for an entire organization. That means that business processes and activities have been defined organization wide. Systems and procedures are in place to collect both actual activity data and budget activity data. Product/service cost and activity information is provided in a format and within a time frame that is useful and relevant for decision making and for tracking operational performance. Finally, a fully implemented ABM information system would have activity information for important activities documented in an activity dictionary.

The level of activity information typical of a completed installation is best illustrated with an example of an activity that might be included in an activity dictionary. The example of the maintain payroll master file activity is common to many organizations and deals with the maintenance of employee information (salary level, marital status, dependents, etc.) needed for payroll and regulatory reporting requirements. Activity information that might be contained in the activity dictionary for this example is outlined in Exhibit 3–1. As illustrated, the level of activity knowledge, information, and understanding includes a clear description of the activity and its associated tasks, costs, outputs/output measures, cost drivers, performance measures, and other attributes. A completed ABM imple-

31

Exhibit 3–1.   Maintain Payroll Master File

Activity Dictionary

Activity	Maintain payroll master file
Business process	Administration of payroll/human resources
Activity number	113
Activity description	Maintain current status of all employee master files
Activity tasks	Receive changes, enter changes, edit changes, and run file
Annual activity cost	$306,000
Activity output	Updated payroll master file
Activity output measure	Number of employees files maintained
Annual activity output	Updated payroll master file for average of 6,600 employees
Cost per unit of output	$46.36 per employee per year
Customer/user of activity	Employee, government agencies
Value added/Nonvalue added	Value added
Performance measurements	Quality: First pass yield on changes
	Cycle time: Employee change request to updated file
	Productivity: Cost per employee file updated or number of files dated per day
Cost drivers	Employee turnover
	Frequency of changes/update
	Changes in federal laws

mentation would have this level of knowledge for all activities being tracked by the system.

This exhibit can also be used to make an important point about the ABM implementation: The amount of detail required for ABM reporting depends on the use and application of the information. In general, more detail and specificity of activities is required for process improvement applications than that required for product/service cost applications. In the exhibit example, activities were specified to the detail and level required to drive and support a process improvement initiative for a payroll department. This might be one of several activities defined for the payroll department and reflects the detail that might be required to manage and control the activities of the department. Had the ABM application been directed only to product/service costing where the objective is to trace costs to products or services, the entire payroll department might have been defined as one activity: pay employees.

In a very large organization a complete ABM installation could take three to five years to complete, whereas in a small company the effort might be accomplished in six months. The total work effort required is a function of several factors, the first of which is the size of the organization, where larger organizations require more time for ABM installation. A second major factor is the starting point. Some organizations have never defined the key and significant processes and activities of their organization, while others may have process flow charts prepared for all significant areas of operation. Starting from scratch is a significant undertaking. The degree of accuracy and granularity required, the frequency of reporting, and the diversity of management needs are additional factors that drive the total implementation effort required. Activity-based management implementations that require highly detailed and precise reporting on a monthly basis will require greater installation efforts than those systems that require less precision and frequency of reporting.

Regardless of how ABM information is used by the organization, the scope of effort, the organization size, or the purpose of implementation, the general steps of implementation are about the same: activities must be specified and defined; activity outputs and measures must be determined; judgments as to activity value must be made; activity performance measures must be established; steps to trace cost to activities and then to the products or services that consume them must be performed; and finally, efforts to develop and install the ongoing activity-based information system must be completed.

BACKGROUND

Through 1995 approximately 3,500 ABC or ABM implementations have been undertaken in North America. This is an estimate based largely on the sale of commercial ABM software systems. Not every software purchase leads to an ABM implementation of substance nor does every ABM implementation use commercial software. However, this estimate is good enough to make a point; i.e., while a large number of organizations have implemented ABM, relative to the use of traditional cost management systems, activity- and process-based management information systems are still in their infancy.

The earliest ABM initiatives were driven by leaders and champions in industry and government willing to experiment and apply the CAM-I conceptual framework of ABC/ABM to the real world. These leaders and champions were the pioneering people and organizations who developed the ABM experience, understanding, knowledge, and skill necessary for success. Most of these organizations began by experimenting with small pilot implementation efforts that included the activities of one department, several departments, a plant, a facility, a company-wide business process, or other piece or unit of the organization. Where the objective was product cost, the focus was on manufacturing overhead.

Until recently, few organizations have undertaken the ABM implementation with the intent of covering the entire organization because the major overhaul of management information systems is expensive and time-consuming. Managers want assurance that the resulting information is useful to them. In addition undertaking implementation for a large organization all at once, without an experience base, would be overwhelming and risky.

COMMON APPROACH TO IMPLEMENTATION

The common approach to initial or pilot implementations for many of these 3,500 organizations is to use a five- to seven-person cross-functional team working during a time frame of three to six months to implement ABM principles, techniques, and methods for some part of the organization. The team is composed of internal people (dedicating 25 to 100% of their time), external consultants, or both.

In a typical pilot installation team members are responsible to prepare an implementation plan to cover the steps and requirements of activity analysis and activity/product costing. Data are gathered through interviews and "crunched" off-line in commercial ABM software or homegrown spreadsheets. A final report containing key findings, observations, recommendations, and next steps is issued to signal the end of the initial pilot phase. Contained in the report appendix are costing assumptions, detailed reports, and activity information.

Report recommendations are generally of two types. The first type has to do with taking whatever actions were identified to improve the performance of the organization. The second type of recommendation has to do with the next steps required to continue the implementation of ABM systems and methods. These next steps might involve either taking on additional parts of the organization or refining and improving the data collection and reporting methods developed in the pilot or both.

Successful pilot efforts lead to additional implementation phases. The knowledge and experience gained from pilot efforts is used to leverage resources and speed implementation, as larger and larger chunks of the organization are included in subsequent phases. This is a very practical approach to getting started. It is senseless to undertake a large-scale ABM implementation without assurance that the resulting information will be useful.

This approach is also practical for another reason. Early ABM visionaries have been willing to share approaches, methodologies, and practices used to conduct pilot ABM installations. The results of some of the earliest implementations directed toward product cost are well known and published. "John Deere Component Works" is covered in a Harvard Business School case study issued in 1989/90. "Siemens Electric Motor Works" and the "Ingersoll Milling Machine Company" case studies are also published works at the Harvard Business School. Case studies now appear on a regular basis, not only in finance trade publications like *Management Accounting, Journal of Cost Management,* and *CFO* magazines but also in publications directed toward the engineering, manufacturing, sales, and quality functions of an organization.

While it is a practical way to get started, the primary weakness with the pilot approach is that it often fails to identify and leave behind efficient systems, procedures, and methods to collect and report activity-based information on an ongoing basis. Without timely, relevant, and ongoing reporting of activity information, the implementation will fail. Another weakness with the pilot approach is the failure to access and identify the needs of the entire organization and to prepare an overall implementation plan for the organization taken as a whole. Pilot efforts to experiment with ABM do not require a company-wide perspective. As a result, pockets of ABM knowledge are independent and isolated.

To achieve its full potential the ABM information system must be integrated with mainstream information systems and the organization's cultures and values. As most organizations have learned, a more holistic approach to implementation is required.

RECOMMENDED IMPLEMENTATION APPROACH

The use, application, and benefit of ABM is documented and generally well published. For most organizations this information, supplemented by analysis, should be adequate to make a decision of whether to implement the total ABM system or to experiment with a pilot effort. When experimenting, use the common approach discussed above. When the goal is to implement an ABM system, a more total approach to implementation is required.

Significant commitments are required to achieve this goal. These commitments are greater than the commitment of resources typically associated with improving an existing system. This difference can be explained in terms of the change in management mind set—from managing cost to managing activities. In addition, implementing ABM requires a willingness to pursue a strategy for improving the activities of the business. Without efforts to improve, resources devoted to implementation are wasted.

In taking a total approach to the ABM implementation, we recommend the following:

1. Do an overall assessment, and prepare an overall implementation plan.

2. Divide and conquer, using a building block approach. First, divide the organization into manageable segments. Then implement each segment in phases, using our four-step model as the basic building block. The steps in the model cover the detailed planning, analysis, data gathering, cost tracing, and documentation necessary to successfully implement the system. The model represents the basic implementation building block and can be applied to all significant portions of the business. It can even be used to conduct a pilot implementation.

3. Develop a cost-effective, ongoing data collection and reporting system.

Overall Assessment and Implementation Plan

Implementing a new ABM information system requires a considerable amount of effort and planning. Like any significant project undertaking, goals must be established, overall requirements must be specified, work must be planned, resources must be identified and earmarked, responsibilities must be assigned, and priorities must be set. An assessment is designed to gather information necessary to prepare and document the overall implementation plan. The result is a preliminary understanding of the requirements, resources, and time lines necessary to fully implement the ABM system. An assessment provides the following:

1. Business process relationship map. Documentation and relationship of key business processes.
2. Preliminary list of key and significant activities. Identification, on a preliminary basis, of major activities, including possible performance measures and potential cost drivers.
3. Preliminary costing of activities and business processes.
4. Estimates of non-value-added activities and costs.
5. Linkage of business processes and activities to the organization's strategic plan.
6. Applicability of ABC product/service costing.
7. Availability of data and information required for the installation.
8. Existing systems capabilities and ability to integrate with activity information.
9. Primary uses of activity-based information.
10. Available resources and implementation requirements.
11. Recommendations for implementation, steps to be taken, and time line.

Typically, assessments take two to six weeks to complete and are performed by consulting firms who specialize in ABM installations. Most organizations will find it difficult to conduct assessments internally because they lack the necessary experience and expertise. The assessment provides a better understanding of needs and requirements prior to commitment of internal resources. It also tends to put the entire organization in perspective; i.e., the whole can be broken down into manageable parts. The assessment also enables management to prioritize and select those initial areas for implementation where efforts will yield the greatest value.

Four-Step Building Block

The general steps involved in an ABM implementation can be expressed in a number of different ways and can be performed in different sequences. Six-, eight-, and twelve-step implementation models have been developed and are in general use. Each model includes steps that involve planning, data gathering, activity analysis, and activity/product costing. Choosing a model is a matter of personal preference and a matter of adapting general models to specific situations. Most models implemented yield similar end results.

The primary difference in the various ABM models is in the area of responsibility for action. The difference is in the viewpoint of how ABM fits the organization. Some view ABM as a management information system only, in which responsibility for action occurs when the information is provided to the decision makers and those responsible for the processes, activities, products, and services of the organization. In other words, activity-based management is a tool to support improvement initiatives and to improve decision making. Others view ABM as a methodology for improvement, in which ABM implementation steps assume a greater level of responsibility for implementing actions, decisions, and changes.

In this book, the viewpoint expressed is that ABM is an information system designed to improve decision making and to drive and support continuous improvement efforts, regardless of the acronym used to describe the initiative. In essence, this is the middle ground between the two viewpoints. Activity-based management information must do more than just support decision making and improvement initiatives. It must drive decision making and improvement. It is not a replacement for existing initiatives like TQM, BPR, benchmarking, or J-I-T. It is an information system that puts teeth into these improvement initiatives, by establishing accountability, measuring results, and setting priorities.

The activity-based implementation model selected for use in this book was simplified to cover the tasks and work required in the area of planning, activity analysis, activity/product costing, documenting results, and data gathering and analysis. This model is illustrated in Exhibit 3–2. The individual tasks involved in planning, activity analysis, activity/product costing, and documenting results are shown under their respective area in the model. The process of data gathering and analysis is ongoing and is an integral part of each step.

The four-step model represents the basic building block of the ABM implementation. The four-step model can be applied on a small scale to a

Exhibit 3–2.   Four-Step ABM Implementation Model

	Data Gathering and Analysis		
Planning	**Activity Analysis**	**Activity/Product Costing**	**Document Results**
Purpose	Specific activities and business processes	Select or develop software	Prepare report
Objectives			Make recommen- dations
Scope		Specify resource drivers	
Time	Outputs and output measures		
Resources		Specify activity drivers	Assign action
Expectations	Value-added analysis		Refine data
Team development	Identify cost drivers	Trace costs	Identify next steps
		Develop costing model	Track improve- ment results
	Activity performance		

specific area of the organization like a department, function, or application; on a large scale to an entire plant, business unit, or facility; and simultaneously to several plants, facilities, departments, or functions. In application, the model is applied over and over until all significant segments of the business have been covered. A summary of each model area follows.

Planning

The four-step model includes detailed planning to define the purpose, objectives, and expectations for each specific ABM building block. A significant part of this planning includes developing a detailed project plan complete with time line and assigned responsibilities, defining the resources required, and selecting specific people to do the work. It also documents the method(s) that will be used to collect data. While planning consumes only a small part of the effort (5 to 15%), it has significant bearing on the outcome.

Activity analysis

Activity analysis is at the heart of the ABM implementation. Specifying activities and processes, identifying cost drivers, documenting outputs and output measures, analyzing activities from a value-added perspective, and developing performance measures each represent major pieces of work that must be performed. Activity analysis can consume as much as 50 to 55% of implementation resources.

Activity/product costing

Activity/product costing is the most mechanical part of the four-step model. It involves documenting the cost tracing methodology and base assumptions. A large part of the work required by this step involves the development or use of a software system to export, import, and accept data necessary to calculate activity and product/service cost. The software system selected or developed as part of this step is often used for the ongoing reporting of activity information. Unless there are significant systems issues or problems, no more than 25 to 30% of project resources should be devoted to this step. For organizations that offer thousands and thousands of products or services and require detailed product/service cost information, a significantly higher percentage of project resources would be required to accomplish this area of work.

Document results

The final step of the ABM four-step implementation model involves documenting the work completed, including results, recommendations, and conclusions. This step is exceedingly important but often neglected. To be successful, action must be taken on the knowledge gained. Decisions regarding next steps are required. To be useful, information on actions to be taken and recommended next steps must be documented. A minimum of 10% of the project effort should be devoted to documenting results.

Data gathering and analysis

Data gathering and analysis is an integral part of each of the four steps reviewed. Planning involves gathering information and data to document the purpose, expectations, and objectives of the implementation effort. Data gathering plays a significant role in the activity analysis. Most of the information required by this step must be gathered from the existing knowledge base in the organization. To complete the activity/product costing step, information about the consumption of resources and activities must be collected and analyzed. Finally, information and data must be analyzed as basis for the recommendations, conclusions, and next steps contained in the documented report. Data gathering and analysis can represent about one-third to one-half of the effort involved in each of the four steps.

Developing a Cost-Effective Data Collection and Reporting System

The final part of the recommended total approach to an ABM implementation is developing an effective, cost-efficient, ongoing data collection and reporting system. The four-step implementation model is designed to provide information about the activities of the organization at a particular point in time. To be useful, activity information must be collected and reported on a continuous basis.

There are two stages to implementing the ongoing ABM information and reporting system. Stage 1 involves establishing the base set of procedures, systems, and methods for ongoing collection of data. Stage 2 relates to ongoing system maintenance requirements.

Implementing procedures, systems, and methods (stage 1)

Under stage 1, procedures, systems, and methods needed for ongoing reporting are implemented. This often involves creating procedures to collect data for the first time, as well as redirecting information and other data from existing sources. Stage 1 is a true "hands-on" period in the organization. It requires extensive use of information services personnel. Data formats and due dates must be established, and the quality requirements expected of data entering the system must be standardized.

Maintaining the activity-based management system (stage 2)

Like any information system, the ABM information system must be maintained on an ongoing basis. Activities change over time. New activities are added. Hopefully, improvement initiatives will eliminate non-value-added activities. Activity performance measures will improve and change over time. New products and services will be added; others will be discontinued. The system must be updated to reflect these changes.

COMPARISON TO OTHER IMPLEMENTATION MODELS

Many organizations offer public ABC/ABM training. All of them have recommended approaches and steps for implementing. For several of these organizations, recommended steps are shown and compared with the four-step model previously presented.

American Productivity & Quality Center

The American Productivity & Quality Center (APQC), based in Houston, Texas, is a nonprofit organization established in 1977 to work with people in organizations to improve productivity, quality, and quality of work life by the following methods:

♦ Providing educational, advisory, and information services of exceptional value.

♦ Researching new methods of improvements on both domestic and international fronts and broadly disseminating its findings.

Since 1987, the Chairman of the APQC, C. Jackson Grayson Jr., and its then president, Carl Thor, directed work to research, test, design, and implement activity-based cost management (ABCM) and performance measurement systems that work with—not against—TQM. Over 5,000 people have attended seminars and conferences that include the eight steps of implementation developed jointly with myself and the APQC. The course emphasis is on the management of activities and the use of activity information to drive and support improvement initiatives. Product/service cost is of secondary importance.

Steps	Planning	Activity Analysis	Activity/ Product Costing	Document Results	Data Gathering
1. Emphasize management commitment	X			X	X
2. Define activities		X			X
3. Determine time period for costing			X		X
4. Trace cost to activities			X		X
5. Determine value/nonvalue added		X			X
6. Define activity outputs/ measures		X			X

Steps	Planning	Activity Analysis	Activity/ Product Costing	Document Results	Data Gathering
7. Identify cost drivers		X			X
8. Calculate product/service cost			X		X

Step 1 of this model emphasizes up-front planning, including the agreement, in advance, that actions will be taken on the basis of knowledge gained. Step 2 calls for the specification of business processes and activities and emphasizes the need to reach consensus on key and significant activities early in the implementation. Step 3 is relatively short and involves a decision as to the period of time under which activities will be costed. Activities could be costed for a month, a quarter, a year, or any other period. In addition, the costing could be done on actual expenditures or budget amounts. Step 4 involves the tracing of cost to the activities specified in step 2. Step 5 involves the analysis of activities and judgments as to whether the activities add value from a customer's (internal or external) perspective. Step 6 involves the identification of activity outputs and activity performance measures for each key and significant activity. Step 7 involves the identification and measurement of cost drivers. Finally, step 8 involves tracing activity costs to products/services or other cost objects, which consume the activities.

Like all ABM implementation models offered in public seminars, the APQC model tends to emphasize the work required in initial or pilot implementations. Insufficient attention is paid to the collection, reliability, application, and reporting of activity data. It also fails to address the importance of integrating activity-based information, data, and knowledge within the organization's structure. These weaknesses were corrected in 1995 when the APQC introduced an advanced course titled "Activity-Based Management (ABM): Systematic Integration" to supplement its updated basics course.

American Management Association

The American Management Association (AMA) is widely recognized for its training capabilities, offering hundreds of courses annually in 29 specific areas of interest. Since 1989, the AMA has offered ABM training in its accounting and controls area of interest. The material used by the AMA was developed by ICMS, Inc., and reflects the philosophies of Tom Pryor and Jim Brimson, each of whom headed the CAM-I cost management task force.

Steps	Planning	Activity Analysis	Activity/ Product Cost	Document Results	Data Gathering
1. Understand significant activities	X	X	X		X
2. Determine activities that need to be changed		X			X
3. Improve activities				X	X
4. Sustain improvement through organizational culture and management information systems	X			X	X

Step 1 is comprehensive and intended to establish a picture of the significant activities as currently performed in the organization. This step involves defining activities and identifying cost drivers, performance measures, activity outputs, and non-value-added activities. Step 2 is primarily analysis work to identify high-priority activities for improvement. Step 3 relates to synchronizing activities within a business process, eliminating wasteful activities, simplifying and improving methods, reducing workload, and matching service levels to customer requirements. Step 4 is designed to sustain improvement by changing the organizational structure, culture, and management information systems through the use of activity-based budgeting, planning, and reporting of activity-based information.

This implementation model emphasis is on process improvement, and to a large degree, it positions ABM as a methodology for improvement. The individual model steps track a common approach to process improvement advocated by many management improvement experts:

1. Determine the "as is" (understand significant activities).
2. Determine the "should be" (determine activities that need to be changed).

3. Change the process (improve activities).

4. Measure the result (sustain improvement).

ABC Technologies, Inc.

Oregon-based ABC Technologies, Inc., is a leading provider of ABM software. Recommended implementation steps are based on building a computer model and emphasize activity analysis and activity/product costing. The planning and documenting results aspects of an ABM implementation are not covered in this material.

Steps	Planning	Activity Analysis	Activity/ Product Cost	Document Results	Data Gathering
1. Identify resources, activities, and cost objects		X			X
2. Define cost assignment paths and specify drivers		X	X		X
3. Enter data			X		
4. Calculate costs			X		

Step 1 encompasses most of the work required by the activity analysis. Step 2 involves the identification and documentation of the methods used to assign, or trace, costs to activities and cost objects. Step 3 involves entering the data required by the model. The final step, performed by the computer, calculates both the cost of activities and the cost objects.

Institute of Management Accountants

Since 1990, the Institute of Management Accountants (formally the National Association of Accountants) has offered a two-day software-based training workshop on implementation of ABC. Developed by Derek J. Sandison and Paul A. Sharman, the eight-step model is based on developing an ABC system and emphasizes the system and reporting aspects of an ABM implementation.

Steps	Planning	Activity Analysis	Activity/ Product Cost	Document Results	Data Gathering
1. Define the problem/ scope	X				X
2. Identify the activities involved and their drivers		X			X
3. Lay out the schematic			X		X
4. Collect related data and rules		X	X		X
5. Build the model			X		X
6. Validate the model with historical data			X		X
7. Interpret the new information		X			X
8. Play scenarios and make recommendations				X	X

Step 1 is directed toward the business issues to be resolved and to prioritize objectives. Step 2 involves determining what activities are important and what drives the activity. Step 3 is used to symbolically document operational flow. The result of step 3 is a schematic of the network of activities representing the defined problem. This schematic is the foundation of model documentation. Step 4 involves the use of existing reports (both operational and financial), expert knowledge from department supervisors, existing standards, or best guesses. Step 5 involves combining the schematic and collected data and rules to create a computer model using modeling software. Step 6 calls for the validation of both operational and financial information. Step 7 is analytical in nature with the intent of understanding what the activity-based information means to the organization. Finally, step 8 involves "what if" analysis and makes specific recommendations for improvements.

SUMMARY

Most ABM implementations conducted to date have been pilot efforts initiated by visionaries and champions in industry and government. These early implementations, directed to parts and pieces of an organization, were designed to validate theory and to test the principles, applications, methods, and procedures in the real world. Evidence was required that these new ABM information systems were better than traditional management information systems. Pilot efforts, often underplanned and underfunded, got the ball rolling but failed to address the overall requirements of the organization and to leave behind the necessary systems, procedures, and reporting required to integrate ABM into the organization.

Judged by significant increases in both the number and the scope of implementations, the evidence indicates that organizations find ABM information valuable to them. Organizations are beginning to aggressively replace traditional information systems with process- or activity-based systems. Pilot efforts are required less frequently, but when they are, the scope of effort is more aggressive. Large-scale ABM projects require a more total approach to implementation, recommended as follows:

1. Perform an overall assessment, and prepare an overall implementation plan.
2. Use the four-step implementation model as the basic building block, and implement it in phases.
3. Put in a cost-effective data collection and reporting system.

The purpose of this chapter was to provide an overview of the implementation requirements, as seen from 40,000 feet. The remainder of this book is at "sea level" and addresses each aspect of the ABM implementation. Activity/product costing will be covered first in Chapter 4. Activity analysis is addressed in Chapter 5. Chapters 6, 7, and 8 cover data gathering, planning, and documenting results, respectively. Chapter 9 offers ten short case study examples of ABM implementations. Chapter 10 reviews the ongoing system requirements. And finally, Chapter 11 is on full integration and challenges the reader with best practices used by world class ABM installations.

4

Activity/Product Costing

The goal is relevance, not precision.

Activity and product/service cost (and/or other cost objects) are fundamental outputs of ABM systems. The methodology of ABC, as compared with traditional cost systems, is based on one fundamental difference. Under ABC, activity and product/service cost (and/or other cost objects) are determined based on the primary principle that activities consume resources (costs). Products and services (cost objects), in turn, consume the activities. This principle is fundamentally different from traditional cost accounting systems whose premise is that product/services consume resources directly, and activity costs are not calculated at all. Activity-based costing is a two-stage tracing methodology: resources (costs) are first traced to activities (stage 1) and activity cost is then traced to products or services (and/or other cost objects), based on their consumption of the activity (stage 2).

THE BASICS

A good illustration of this new ABC methodology, as developed by ABC Technologies, Inc., a leading supplier of ABC software, is set forth in Exhibit 4–1. This illustration was adapted from CAM-I and shows the flow of cost

---

Exhibit 4–1.   Cost Assignment under ABC

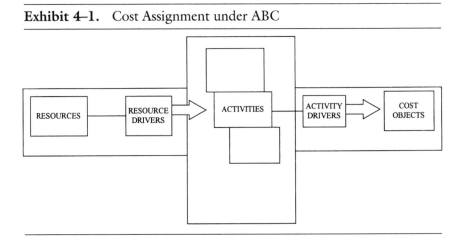

---

assignment horizontally. Resources (costs) are assigned to activities. Activity cost is then assigned to cost objects.

As illustrated in Exhibit 4–1 above, there are five basic components to the activity-based cost assignment methodology: resources, resource drivers, activities, activity drivers, and cost objects.

Resources

Resources are what organizations spend their money on—the categories of costs that are recorded in the general ledger. *Resource* is defined as an economic element that is applied or used in the performance of activities. Salaries and materials, for example, are resources used in the performance of activities. Additional examples of resources include travel, rent, depreciation, utilities, insurance, and supplies. Most ABC systems currently exclude costs like income taxes and interest expense that are not used in the performance of activities.

Resource Drivers

Resource drivers are the basis for tracing resources to activities. *Resource driver* is defined as a measure of the quantity of resources consumed by an activity. An example of a resource driver is the percentage of total square feet of space occupied by an activity. This factor is used to trace a portion of the cost of operating the facilities to the activity.

Examples of common resource drivers for salaries/wages, rent, equipment, depreciation, and utilities include the following:

Resource	Resource Driver
Salaries	Percentage of people's time spent on each activity.
	Headcount assignment.
	Hours spent on each activity.
Rent/facility costs	Square feet of facility consumed by each activity.
	Cubic feet of facility consumed by each activity.
Equipment depreciation	Specific analysis to associate equipment use to each activity.
	Machine time by activity.
Utilities (electric)	Kilowatt hours consumption by activity.
	Square feet of facility.

Activities

Activities, as previously defined in Chapter 1, represent work performed in an organization. The cost of activities is determined by tracing resources to activities using the resource drivers. An example of how the salaries of a receiving department of a manufacturing company might be traced to receiving department activities is illustrated in Exhibit 4–2. In this example, the resource is receiving department salaries. The activities are as follows: receive materials, unload trucks, move material, schedule receipts, expedite material, and resolve vendor errors. The resource driver is a percentage of people's time devoted to each receiving department activity. While percentage of people's time was selected as the resource driver in this example, as an alternative, the head count of people assigned to each activity or the hours devoted to each activity could have been used as the resource driver.

Assuming that salaries were the only resource of the receiving department, calculating the cost of receiving department activities would be quite simple. All that is required is to multiply the percentage of people's

Exhibit 4-2. Resource Driver Example

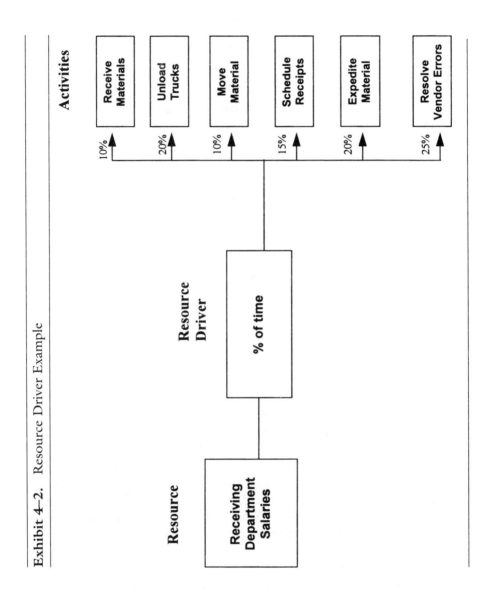

time (resource driver) by the salary amount. If receiving department salaries totaled $1 million, the cost of each activity would be as follows:

Receive materials	$100,000
Unload trucks	200,000
Move material	100,000
Schedule receipts	150,000
Expedite material	200,000
Resolve Vendor Errors	250,000
Total	$1,000,000

In practice, a single resource and resource driver would be rare. The receiving department of a large organization is likely to have multiple resources and resource drivers. Total activity cost would be determined by tracing each resource (using an appropriate resource driver) to the receiving department activities. Once determined, activity costs can be traced to cost objects using activity drivers.

Activity Drivers

Like a resource driver that is used to trace resources to activities, an activity driver is used to trace activity costs to cost objects. *Activity driver* is defined as a measure of the frequency and intensity of the demands placed on activities by cost objects. An activity driver is used to assign costs to cost objects. It represents a line item on the bill of activities for a product or customer. An example is the number of part numbers, which is used to measure the consumption of material-related activities by each product, material type, or component. The number of customer orders measures the consumption of order-entry activities by each customer. Sometimes an activity driver is used as an indicator of the output of an activity, such as the number of purchase orders prepared by the purchasing activity.

This simply means that activity costs are traced to cost objects based on activity usage (consumption). The CAM-I definition provides an example of an activity driver, number of part numbers, used to trace material-related activities to cost objects. In this example, material-related activities might include receive raw materials, inspect raw materials, and store parts. Assuming that each part number represents a received, inspected, and stored part, the number of part numbers could be used to trace each activity cost (or all three combined) to cost objects. Products and/or other cost objects that have the most parts (part numbers) will have a greater portion of material-related activity costs.

When identifying and selecting activity drivers, match the activity to the *activity level,* which is defined as a description of how an activity is used by a cost object or other activity. Some activity levels describe the cost object that uses the activity and the nature of its use. These levels include activities that are traceable to the product (i.e., unit-level, batch-level, and product-level costs), to the customer (customer-level costs), to a market (market-level costs), to a distribution channel (channel-level costs), and to a project, such as a research and development project (project-level costs).

Tips for identifying activity drivers include the following:

♦ Pick activity drivers that correlate with the actual consumption of the activity.

♦ Minimize the number of unique drivers. Cost and complexity are directly correlated with the number of drivers.

♦ Pick activity drivers that encourage improved performance.

♦ Pick activity drivers that are already available and/or have a low cost of collection.

Cost Object

Cost objects, as previously defined in Chapter 1, can be any customer, product, service, contract, project, or other work unit for which a separate cost measurement is desired. The most common cost object is product or service cost. Activity drivers are used to trace activity costs to cost objects. An example of how an activity of a sales department might be traced to customer segments (cost object) is illustrated in Exhibit 4–3.

In this example, the activity of the sales department is make sales calls. The activity driver is the number of sales calls. If the objective was to determine the selling cost associated with customer segments, then the cost objects might be large customers, medium-sized customers, and small customers. Assume that the make sales calls activity costs $250,000 and was the only activity of the department. If the total sales calls made were 5,000, of which 1,000 were made on large customers, 500 on medium customers, and 3,500 on small customers, the cost of each customer segment would be as follows:

Exhibit 4-3. Activity Driver Example

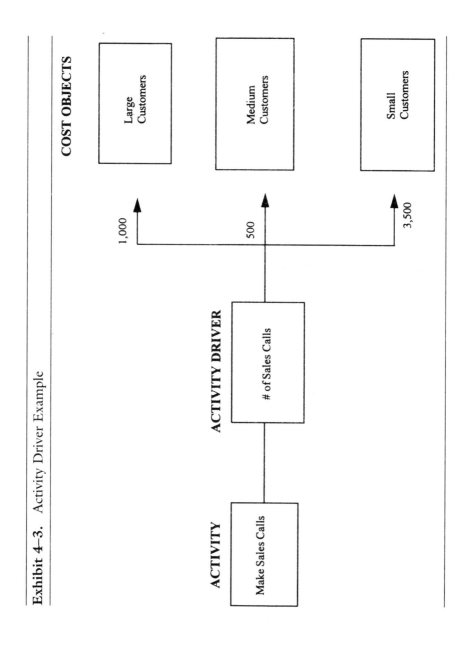

Large Customers	$ 50,000
Medium Customers	25,000
Small Customers	175,000
Total Activity Cost	$250,000

Again, like the Resource Driver Example (refer to Exhibit 4–2), single activities and activity drivers do not exist. It is only by tracing other sales department activities like prepare proposals, answer inquires, and take orders that the total cost for each of the customer segments identified as cost objects could be determined.

The foregoing examples were intended to be simple and to demonstrate the basic concepts of ABC. Applications of these concepts in practice can be quite complex. Even the simplest of ABC applications could involve 5 to 10 resources, 25 or more activities, and 10 to 25 cost objects. That is why it is important to resist the urge for perfection by defining activities and drivers at too detailed a level, especially in the early stages of implementation. The goal of ABM is to provide relevant information useful for decision making, measuring performance, and effecting improvement. Do not give up relevance for precision.

In a survey conducted jointly by the APQC and CAM-I of over 150 companies known to have best practices in the area of ABM, the following information was learned:

1. About forty percent of respondents indicated the total number of activities for their organization was between 101 and 250; thirty percent had 26 to 100 activities.

2. Thirty-two percent of respondents indicated the total cost objects as between 26 and 100. Two companies identified over 10,000 cost objects.

3. Forty percent of respondents indicated the number of activity drivers as 6 to 15, and forty-five percent had identified five to ten resource drivers.

Computers and commercially available ABC software can take much of the drudgery, difficulty, and complexity out of using ABC methods. These commercial software applications provide a structured way of identifying, entering, storing, and calculating the data required for ABC.

ABC APPLICATION EXAMPLE

A simple example can be used to (1) illustrate the difference in traditional costing and ABC, (2) demonstrate a more complete application of these new ABC methods in a product cost application, and (3) point out a flaw in traditional cost systems. In this example, a company, XYZ Corporation, makes only two products: product A and product B. Manufacturing operations consist of assembling (direct labor) components parts (raw material) into a finished product for sale to customers. Overhead at the XYZ Corporation is three times the direct labor cost and consists of a storage warehouse, some inspection equipment, and people who receive, inspect, and store the component parts.

Product cost at XYZ Corporation, using traditional product costing methods, would include the direct material and direct labor of product A and product B, plus $3 of overhead for each $1 of direct labor. For purposes of this example, assume that costs and units manufactured are the same for both products, as follows:

	Product A	Product B
Direct material (component parts)	$500,000	$500,000
Direct labor (assembly)	300,000	300,000
Overhead (300% of direct labor)	900,000	900,000
Total product cost	$1,700,000	$1,700,000
Units manufactured	17,000	17,000
Cost per unit	$100	$100

XYZ corporation is considering a change in its raw material supplier of component parts for product B. The new supplier will sell the components at the same price but with a higher level of tolerance that makes the assembly of the components easier. So much easier, in fact, that the labor required for assembly can be reduced enough to cut the direct labor workforce for product B in half and reduce the direct labor cost from $300,000 to $150,000. For purpose of example, assume that changing the raw material supplier requires additional overhead costs of storage space and inspection personnel, which completely offset the direct labor reductions. All of these additional overhead costs are for product B. Therefore, there is no change in the total cost of product B.

While no cost savings result from the change in supplier, XYZ Corporation believes the new components will increase the reliability of the products and thus makes the change in suppliers. Concurrent with this decision, the new overhead costs are added, and direct labor is reduced. Several months later, cost accountants at XYZ Corporation update direct labor and overhead accounts for the change. The new overhead rate is 433% based on the new total labor amount of $450,000 and the new overhead amount of $1,950,000. Product costs for A and B are now calculated as follows:

	Product A	**Product B**
Direct material (component parts)	$500,000	$500,000
Direct labor (assembly)	300,000	150,000
Overhead at 433%	1,300,000	650,000
Total product cost	$2,100,000	$1,300,000
Units manufactured	17,000	17,000
Cost per unit	$124	$76

In reality, costs have not changed. For product B we simply use less direct labor and more overhead. Yet traditional product cost determination indicates that the cost of product A has increased 24% and that the cost of product B has decreased 24%. Herein lies the flaw in traditional thinking: the assumption that overhead is a function of direct labor. In some businesses and industries it is, in others it is not.

In using ABC methodologies in this example at XYZ Corporation, overhead costs would not be allocated to products A and B based on direct labor. Instead, overhead costs (resources) would first be traced to overhead activities, then traced to either product A or product B, based on each product's consumption of the overhead activities. Resources are first traced to activities. This is known as *resource cost assignment,* defined as the process by which cost is attached to activities. This process requires the assignment of cost from general ledger accounts to activities using resource drivers. For example, the chart of accounts may list information services at a plant level. It then becomes necessary to trace (assuming that tracing is practical) or to allocate (when tracing is not practical) the cost of information services to the activities that benefit from the information services by means of appropriate resource drivers. It may be necessary to set up intermediate activity cost pools to accumulate related costs from various resources before the assignment can be made.

In this example for XYZ Corporation, assume there are only three overhead activities: receive raw materials, inspect raw materials, and store raw materials. Total overhead cost ($1,950,000) includes rent on the warehouse ($400,000), depreciation of equipment ($550,000), and salaries of people ($1,000,000) who perform the overhead activities of receive, inspect, and store raw materials.

Using the ABC methodology, the cost of rent, salaries, and depreciation resources are traced to the three overhead activities using resource drivers. In this example, the resource driver selected for salaries was the head count of people assigned to each activity. For warehouse rent, the resource driver selected was the square footage of the facility devoted to each activity. For depreciation of equipment, the resource driver selected was based on the specific use of equipment because some equipment was used in storage, some in receiving, and some in inspection. Sometimes it is helpful to group similar costs to facilitate tracing. Payroll costs are often grouped with payroll-related costs like payroll taxes and employee benefits. This is known as establishing a *resource cost pool,* defined as a grouping of cost elements.

After analysis and data gathering, the resource driver quantities consumed by each activity were determined to be as follows:

	Resource Drivers		
Activity	Number of Personnel (Salaries)	Square Footage (Rent)	Specific Dollar Use (Equipment)
Receive raw materials	2	10,000	$50,000
Inspect raw materials	12	15,000	400,000
Store raw materials	6	75,000	100,000
Total	20	100,000	$550,000

Activity cost is calculated by applying the resource drivers to the three overhead cost resources of salaries, rent, and depreciation and by totaling the pieces. The resultant activity costs are set forth in Exhibit 4-4. The exhibit indicates the amount of cost traced for each resource to each activity. Salary costs ($1,000,000) traced to activities based on head count results in the following:

1. Ten percent of the cost (2 out of 20 people) being traced to the activity of receive raw materials.

2. Sixty percent of the cost (12 out of 20 people) being traced to the activity of inspect raw materials.

3. The remaining 30% (6 out of 20 people) traced to the activity of store raw materials.

Rent ($400,000), traced to activities based on square footage, results in 75% of this resource being traced to the activity of store raw materials because that activity occupies or consumes 75% of the facility (75,000 square feet out of a total of 100,000 square feet). The activities of receive raw materials and inspect raw materials each receive a portion of rent costs based on their portion of square footage consumed, 10% and 15%, respectively. Equipment depreciation, traced to activities based on specific dollar use, does not require any additional calculations.

Activity costing is now complete, and the activity costs of receive raw materials ($190,000), inspect raw materials ($1,060,000), and store raw materials ($700,000) can be traced to either product A or product B, based on the consumption (use) of the activity.

Exhibit 4-4. Overhead Activity Costs for XYZ Corporation

	Receive Raw Material	Inspect Raw Material	Store Raw Material	Total
Salaries	$100,000	$600,000	$300,000	$1,000,000
Rent	40,000	60,000	300,000	400,000
Equipment depreciation	50,000	400,000	100,000	550,000
Total	$190,000	$1,060,000	$700,000	$1,950,000

Tracing activity costs to products or services using activity drivers is known as *activity cost assignment,* defined as the process in which the cost of activities is attached to cost objects using activity drivers. Activity drivers are used to assign activity costs to cost objects like products or services. Activity costs are traced/assigned to products/services or other cost objects based on the consumption of activity outputs.

Activity tracing could be accomplished by tracing the output of a single activity to its product/service or other cost object. Activity tracing could also be accomplished by combining similar activities and selecting a representative output for the combined group and tracing this representative output to its product/service or cost object. In addition, activity costs can be traced to products without reference to activity outputs. For example, the number of transactions processed (where transactions could be related to cost objects) might be an acceptable way to trace multiple activities of the accounting department to products/services or cost objects. Finally, activity tracing could be accomplished by using a *surrogate activity driver,* defined as an activity driver that is not descriptive of an activity but that is closely correlated to the performance of the activity. The use of a surrogate activity driver should reduce measurement costs without significantly increasing the costing bias. The number of production runs, for example, is not descriptive of the material disbursing activity, but the number of production runs may be used as an activity driver if material disbursements coincide with production runs.

Surrogate activity drivers are particularly useful in the early stages of ABM implementation. There are several reasons for this. First, the surrogate information is more likely to be available. Activity output is not always collected. In addition, in the early stages of implementation it is important to get feedback about the usefulness and relevance of ABM information. Using available surrogate information will enable quickly tracing costs and producing initial reports and information for review and comment. Finally, surrogate activity drivers often provide adequate and relevant information. No additional work is required.

In the XYZ Corporation example, the three activities of receive raw materials, inspect raw materials, and store raw materials will individually be traced to cost objects product A and product B, using activity outputs as the activity driver. The output of the receive raw materials activity is components received. If the total components received was 3,000 and two-thirds of the components received were for product A, then product

A should get two-thirds of the receive raw materials activity, as shown in the following:

	Components Received	Percentage of Total
Product A	2,000	67%
Product B	1,000	33%
Total	3,000	100%

The activity driver for the inspect raw materials activity might be number of inspections completed, where the activity output is a completed inspection. If most of the inspections are for product B components because of the higher tolerances, then product B should get most of the inspect raw materials activity cost, even though it has fewer component parts. If the total of completed inspections was 1,100, of which 1,000 were for product B, then product B should get 91% of the inspect raw materials activity, as shown in the following:

	Components Inspected	Percentage of Total
Product A	100	9%
Product B	1,000	91%
Total	1,100	100%

For the store raw materials activity where the output is a stored component, the activity driver might be the number of stored components. As an alternative, the activity driver might be the percentage of the total storage space. Either of these activity drivers could be used to trace activity costs to products A and B. In selecting activity drivers, it is quite common to have alternatives. Judgments and analysis are required to select the best activity driver, given the situation. This analysis is known as *activity driver analysis,* defined as the identification and evaluation of the activity drivers used to trace the cost of activities to cost objects. Activity driver analysis may also involve selecting activity drivers with a potential for cost reduction.

In the XYZ Corporation example there are many alternative activity drivers. The receive raw materials activity could have been traced to products A and B based on the number of boxes received, number of pounds received, or number of vendor orders received. The inspect raw materials activity might have been traced on the basis of equivalent inspections, where complex inspections might count as three equivalent inspection units, and a simple sight inspection might count as one equivalent unit. All three activities could have been traced on a combined basis using the number of component parts used in each product. The selection of activity drivers is specific to the situation and the individual organization. Good judgment, based on identification and analysis of alternatives, is required.

Using the number of stored components as the activity driver for the store raw materials activity and assuming that the number of components stored, on average, was the same for products A and B, the activity cost would be split evenly between the products as follows:

	Components Stored	**Percentage of Total**
Product A	12,000	50%
Product B	12,000	50%
Total	24,000	100%

Total activity-based cost for products A and B can be completed by applying the activity drivers to the three activities of receive raw materials, inspect raw materials, and store raw materials and including the resultant costs with the direct material and labor. Displaying product cost under activity-based costing is often done with a *bill of activities,* defined as a listing of the activities required (and, optionally, the associated costs of the resources consumed) by a product or other cost object. The bill of activities, displaying total product cost for the two products of XYZ Corporation, is shown in Exhibit 4–5.

For XYZ Corporation, raw material and assembly labor were deemed to be *direct cost,* defined as a cost that is traced directly to an activity or a cost object. For example, the material issued to a particular work order or the engineering time devoted to a specific product are direct costs to the work orders or products. Direct costs of material and labor were already

Exhibit 4–5. ABC Product Costing for XYZ Corporation

Description	Product A	Product B
Direct material (component parts)	$500,000	$500,000
Direct labor (assembly)	300,000	150,000
Receive raw material	127,000	63,000
Inspect raw material	95,000	965,000
Store raw material	350,000	350,000
Total product cost	$1,372,000	$2,028,000
Units manufactured	17,000	17,000
Cost per unit	$81	$119

associated with products A and B under the traditional cost system. Additional activity-based cost tracing was not required.

The bill of activities shown in Exhibit 4–5 includes products A and B portionate share of the three overhead activities. Based on the activity driver components received, product A received two-thirds of the cost of the receive raw materials activity, and product B received one-third. Based on the activity driver completed inceptions, product B got 91% of the inspect raw materials activity, and product A received the remaining 9%. Because the activity driver, number of stored components, was the same for both products A and B, the cost of the store raw materials activity was split evenly between the products.

COMPARISON BETWEEN TRADITIONAL
AND ACTIVITY-BASED COSTING

A comparison of traditional and activity-based product cost, determined after the company made a change in its raw material supplier, is as follows:

	Cost Per Unit	
	Product A	Product B
Traditional	$124	$76
Activity-based costing	$81	$119

Like many examples and comparisons of traditional cost with ABC, this example also took the best of ABC and the worst of traditional costing. In application, cost accounting managers have recognized this overhead allocation problem for years. In traditional cost accounting systems, it is not unusual for cost accountants to break overhead costs into cost pools for allocation on basis other than direct labor. Practitioners of ABC can be overwhelmed by the task of tracing 50 to 100 individual activities to products. They find it useful to group similar kinds of activities to facilitate tracing of cost and to use surrogate drivers. In many cases, overhead pools and activity groups, calculated independently, begin to bear resemblance. In fact, many organizations have developed their traditional cost systems to the point where they may be applying some ABC methods and techniques.

The primary area of difference between calculating cost under the two methods is overhead. Direct costs are the same under either method. The method of allocating/tracing overhead to products/services or other cost objects is what gives wide differences in total product/service costs determined under the two methods. These differences can be as high as ±50%. Years ago, when direct labor and direct material often represented 80% or more of total product cost, differences in the two methods would not have been so pronounced. Today, many organizations spend less than 5% of their total resources on direct labor, and allocating cost on the basis of a relatively insignificant cost is not appropriate.

Another difference is that traditional cost accounting generally determines product cost in accordance with GAAP and *cost accounting standards,* defined as (1) rules promulgated by the Cost Accounting Standards Board of the U.S. Government to ensure contractor compliance in the accounting of government contracts and (2) a set of rules issued by any of several authorized organizations or agencies, such as the American Institute of Certified Public Accountants (AICPA) or the Association of Chartered Accountants (ACA), dealing with the determination of costs to be allocated, inventoried, or expensed. These standards require product cost to include only costs of resources directly associated with manufacturing the product. Costs and resources associated with the sale, distribution, and administration of products are ignored in traditional calculations of product/service cost. The primary reason for exclusion of costs other than manufacturing is because they cannot be included in the inventory amount reported under GAAP in external financial statements.

Under ABC all costs associated with a product/service or other cost object can be traced to determine the true cost of a product or service sold and distributed in a particular market or to a customer. Activity-based product costing can still be used for external reporting requirements under GAAP by simply breaking the calculation into two parts, with a subtotal that includes activities and costs allowed by GAAP.

Some people question whether activity-based product cost is in accordance with GAAP and are reluctant to change from traditional methods. The GAAP requires inventory to be stated at the lower of cost or market; it does not specify a particular method of determining cost. Traditional cost accounting systems that substantially misstate cost, like the example from XYZ Corporation, may not be in accordance with GAAP because their systems do not accurately portray cost. Therefore, inventories may not be stated at the lower of cost or market nor are they in accordance with GAAP.

Another difference between traditional and activity-based costing is the historical orientation. It is not unusual for an organization to use actual historical cost as the basis for developing manufacturing cost standards. These historical costs often include rework, duplication, waste, redundancy, and inefficiency. Accepting historical costs as a given and reflecting these costs in standards does not support continuous improvement. In a competitive situation, where competitors have been proactive in eliminating waste and improving activities, an organization can go out of business while meeting its standards. While activity-based costs are also calculated using historical resource costs, the orientation is different. Proponents of ABC are concerned about future competitive positions and use historical cost only as a baseline for improvement.

Costs can be either allocated or traced to activities and cost objects. Under traditional cost systems most costs are allocated. In ABC allocated cost is referred to as *indirect cost,* defined as the cost that is allocated—as opposed to being traced—to an activity or a cost object. For example, the costs of supervision or heat may be allocated to an activity on the basis of direct labor hours. With ABC, most costs are traced. Tracing is always preferred because cause and effect are established. But tracing, even under ABC, is not always practical or possible. Some costs just cannot be traced. For some costs, allocations are required. The differences between tracing and allocation are contained in their definitions.

Tracing is defined as the assignment of cost to an activity or a cost object using an observable measure of the consumption of resources by the activity or cost object. Tracing is generally preferred to allocation if the data exist or can be obtained at a reasonable cost. For example, if a company's cost accounting system captures the cost of supplies according to which activity uses the supplies, the costs may be traced—as opposed to allocated—to the appropriate activities.

Allocation is defined as (1) an apportionment or distribution and (2) a process of assigning cost to an activity or cost object when a direct measure does not exist. For example, assigning the cost of power to a machine activity by means of machine hours is an allocation, because machine hours is an indirect measure of power consumption. In some cases, allocations can be converted to tracing by incurring additional measurement costs. Instead of using machine hours to allocate power consumption, for example, a company can place a power meter on machines to measure actual power consumption.

In deciding whether to allocate or trace, practicality is the rule of the day. Installing power meters at each machine as a way to trace, rather than allocate, power consumption directly to activities and cost objects might not be a practical thing to do, especially if power consumption was not a significant cost. Keep in mind *traceability,* which is defined as the ability to assign a cost by means of causal relationship directly to an activity or a cost object in an economically feasible way. Consider traceability in all judgments made as to whether to trace or allocate a cost. As a rule of thumb, most organizations should strive to trace 70% of resource costs to activities and cost objects. The remainder can be allocated.

SUMMARY

The effort expended in activity/product costing is a function of the level of accuracy required. The higher the requirement for accuracy, the more analysis, detail, data, and information are needed. At some point, the level of accuracy begins to diminish, in spite of the detail and analysis. Activity-based management systems are built around the notion of relevance as opposed to precision. Unlike traditional cost systems that often carry out product/service cost 3, 4, or 5 decimal points, when the numbers on the left-hand side of the decimal point are wrong, the ABC goal is a relevant cost sometimes expressed within a range. Traditional cost systems that calculate a widget's cost as $12.532 are not particularly useful when we do not know whether the dollar amount is 10 or 15.

The frequency of reporting information under ABM is largely a function of the system's purpose and use. It would not be unusual to report cost and performance measurements on an hourly basis for some activities, yet on a quarterly basis for others. The reporting of activity performance on both an hourly and a quarterly basis could exist within the framework of an ABM, assuming that the activity performance is measured and reported to line managers hourly and summarized in a quarterly report to top management. Product costing might be performed annually as the basis for standard product costs. Updates would not occur any more frequently then updates to traditional systems.

The application of ABC has evolved considerably from its original product cost roots. The ABC methodologies can be used to provide accurate cost on projects, services, contracts, customers, and distribution channels. The methodology is the same: trace resource cost to activities then trace activity cost to cost objects. Activity-based costing is largely mechanical, providing that the necessary data and information required for tracing are available. Commercially available ABM software makes the work of "number crunching" easier and provides a structure for collecting, storing, and reporting activity-based cost information.

5

Activity Analysis

Where the rubber meets the road.

Nothing in an ABM implementation is more important than activity analysis, which is where the critical work gets completed. Activity analysis involves defining business processes and activities together with related outputs, cost drivers, customers or users, and performance measures. Activity analysis is the stage where judgments are made about the value of activities to the organization. These are important areas to the ABM implementation.

Activity analysis is defined as the identification and description of activities in an organization. Activity analysis involves determining what activities are done within a department [or area of business], how many people perform the activities, how much time they spend performing the activities, what resources are required to perform the activities, what operational data best reflect the performance of the activities, and what value the activity has for the organization. Activity analysis is accomplished by means of interviews, questionnaires, and reviews of physical records of work.

The steps involved in activity analysis include the following:

1. Define business processes and specify key and significant activities.
2. Define activity outputs/measures.

3. Identify the customer/user of activity outputs.

4. Perform value-added analysis.

5. Identify cost drivers.

6. Determine activity performance measures and goals.

7. Define other activity attributes.

8. Gather activity data required for activity/product costing.

Step 1 must be completed first; however, steps 2 through 8 need not follow the order given. It is not necessary to have defined activity outputs before identifying cost drivers. Nor is it necessary to know if an activity is value added or nonvalue added before determining activity attributes. Performance measures of activity performance can be determined without knowing the cost drivers or whether the activity is value added. In some cases it is even helpful to complete part of the activity analysis and then move to activity/product costing to get a preliminary look at activity costs.

As an example, an organization may wish to specify activities (step 1) and then gather preliminary data (step 8) on resource drivers, such as how people spend their time, and make a preliminary estimate of activity cost. Preliminary estimates of activity cost can be helpful in reaching decision and consensus on key and significant activities. Low-cost activities might be combined with other activities or deleted all together. Conversely, the costing of activities might identify activities that are candidates for decomposition or further breakdown. In fact, as long as the necessary data required for activity and product/service costing is available, the costing work can be done concurrent with the activity analysis.

While steps 2 through 8 can be performed in any order, we recommend the order of steps given. By first determining the output of the activity (step 2) and then its customer (step 3), a better judgment can be made about activity value (step 4). Activities that produce no useful output or produce outputs where a user or customer cannot be identified are candidates for a non-value-added classification. Cost driver identification (step 5) is more effective when specifically directed toward value-added or non-value-added activities, because the improvement objectives are different. When identifying cost drivers for a non-value-added activity, the objective is to identify cost drivers that can be eliminated. The goal is to eliminate or reduce the activity as much as possible. A cost driver analysis of a value-added activity is directed toward identifying those cost drivers that can be optimized.

For several reasons, step 6 is best done after steps 1 through 5 have been completed. The first reason is that by knowing the customer or user of the activity output, the customer can be involved in determining the appropriate and important measures of activity performance. Who would be better than the customer or user to know what is important to measure? The second reason is that knowing if an activity is value added or nonvalue added aids in determining what to measure. It is not important to measure the efficiency of a non-value-added activity, where the objective is to eliminate the activity all together. Finally, activity performance goals are best determined after cost drivers have been identified. Cost drivers that can be influenced in the short term should be reflected in short-term activity performance goals. Alternatively, based on cost driver identification, it might be determined that the cost drivers cannot be influenced in the short term. Therefore, short- or medium-term improvement goals would not be appropriate.

Step 7 is best left until the end of the analysis, unless there is a specific need for the information. Generally, this work can be performed fairly quickly. Step 8 is ongoing and is completed at many different points in the activity analysis. A discussion of each of these steps follows.

DEFINE BUSINESS PROCESSES AND SPECIFY ACTIVITIES

The first step to activity analysis is to define and specify business processes and activities. This is easier said than done, and stumbling blocks await the implementor. One of the stumbling blocks occurs when activities are defined at too detailed a level, and the resulting activity specification includes thousands and thousands of activities. Especially in initial and early stages of ABM implementations it is difficult to manage this much data. Equally dangerous is defining activities at too high a level such that the resulting activity specification includes only 20 to 25 key activities for an entire organization. In this case, activity information is aggregated too broadly for action and decision making.

A major reason for these stumbling blocks is that the word activity means different things to different people. Some see activities as composed of tasks. Others see tasks composed of activities. Still others see activities as composed of processes. It is really a matter of how different people define the hierarchy of work flows, or processes, of the organization.

Often the word process is the problem itself. Most organizations use the term process loosely. Terms like business process, subprocess, department process, major process, primary process, minor process, secondary process, activity, subactivity, task, step, core process, and supporting process are used interchangeable to describe a work sequence/process. The word process applies to making a phone call where each number must be dialed in sequence to reach the intended party. It equally applies to developing new products for a Fortune 500 company where major pieces of work must be done in sequence, or sequentially, to develop a new product. Both meet the definition of the word process.

What is important is to establish a hierarchy of process and clearly communicate, by example, the use/application of process. A simple hierarchy of business process, activity, and task works well. Business processes can be further grouped as core processes or supporting processes. For example, new product development might be the business process. Key and significant activities associated with this business process might be research market, define customer requirements, develop prototypes, and test prototypes. Tasks under the research market activity might include conducting surveys, analyzing and collecting data, and developing customer procurement profiles.

In the activity-based world, establishing a hierarchy of process is known as *functional decomposition* and identifies the activities performed in the organization. It yields a hierarchical representation of the organization and shows the relationship between the different levels of the organization and its activities. For example, a hierarchy may start with the division and move down through the plant, function, process, activity, and task levels.

As a rule of thumb, most business organizations should be able to describe their business with 8 to 16 business processes. Key and significant activities might average 10 to 20 for each business process. An organization with 16 business processes each composed of 12 activities would have a shade under 200 activities total, a manageable number.

Activity Definition Options

In defining activities and business processes, two options are generally used:

1. Top-down. First specify business processes, then specify activities. Using this option, business process are defined first. Key and significant activities are then identified for each business process.

2. Bottom-up. First specify activities, then arrange into business processes. Under this option, activities are specified in detail for the departments and areas covered by the activity analysis. Activity inputs and outputs are used to link activities into business processes.

While either option method ultimately results in adequate definitions of business processes and activities, the combination of both options works best. Concurrent efforts to define the important business processes of the organization, together with a more detailed effort to understand what work (activities) are actually performed, when combined, will result in well-defined and understood business processes and activities.

Top-down approach to defining business processes and activities

Many ABM practitioners find the top-down option valuable because of the "big picture" understanding and immediate gratification that comes from reaching consensus on the major business processes of the organization. The value of the top-down approach can be enhanced by developing a business process relationship map to both document business processes and indicate their relationship to one another. A good business process relationship map provides a visual picture of the business processes and their relationships, without undue complexity.

Business process relationship maps, often completed on an $8\frac{1}{2} \times 11$ piece of paper, are useful for communication and can be used as the blueprint for the entire ABM implementation. They serve as a predetermined framework under which the activities can be captured. The top-down approach to defining business processes and activities is complete when all of the key and significant activities have been specified for each of the business processes.

There are several tools available and useful for defining business processes and activities, especially for those doing it the first time. While most organizations see their operations as completely unique, an outsider who has had the opportunity to see many different industries sees more similarities than differences. Every business has to develop new services and products, to produce the product or provide the service, to market and sell, and to deliver the product or service to its customer. Each business is supported by accounting, human resources, data processing, and other administrative functions who perform similar activities, regardless of industry or size. Generic frameworks for business processes and activities, when adapted to the specific organization, serve as an excellent starting point for business process and activity specification. These generic frameworks are valuable tools.

In 1985, Michael E. Porter introduced the Value Chain, as a tool to systematically examine all the activities a firm performs and how well they interact ("Competitive Advantage," *The Free Press*, 1985). The purpose of Mr. Porter's value chain was to identify sources of competitive advantage. *Value chain* is defined as the set of activities required to design, procure, produce, market, distribute, and service a product or service or, as in Mr. Porter's words, "Every firm is a collection of activities to design, produce, market, distribute and service a product." This tool is useful and relevant to defining business process and activities for an organization by providing a generic set of business processes and activities that apply to most organizations.

The generic value chain (ibid., 37), developed by Mr. Porter, grouped activities (i.e., business processes) as primary or support. Primary activities are subdivided generically as inbound logistics, operations, outbound logistics, marketing, and sales and service. Support activities (i.e., business processes) are subdivided as firm infrastructure, human resource management, technology development, and procurement. These generic categories of activities, or business processes, apply to most businesses and can be the starting point for business process definition when tailored to the terminology and nomenclature of the particular organization. Distinct activities (i.e., activities), defined by Mr. Porter, as associated with the generic activity categories are as follows:

Primary

- ◆ Inbound logistics: Activities associated with receiving, storing, and disseminating inputs to the product, such as material handling, warehousing, inventory control, vehicle scheduling, and returns to suppliers.

- ◆ Operations: Activities associated with transforming inputs into the final product form, such as machining, packaging, assembly, equipment maintenance, testing, printing, and facility operations.

- ◆ Outbound logistics: Activities associated with collecting, storing, and physically distributing the product to buyers, such as finished goods warehousing, material handling, delivery vehicle operation, order processing, and scheduling.

- ◆ Marketing and sales: Activities associated with providing a means by which buyers can purchase the product and inducing them to do so, such as advertising, promotion, sales force, quoting, channel selection, channel relations, and pricing.

♦ Service: Activities associated with providing service to enhance or maintain the value of the product, such as installation, repair, training, parts supply, and product adjustment.

Support

♦ Firm infrastructure: Firm infrastructure consists of a number of activities, including general management, planning, finance, accounting, legal, government affairs, and quality management. Infrastructure, unlike other support activities, usually supports the entire chain and not individual activities.

♦ Human resource management: Human resource management consists of activities involved in the recruiting, hiring, training, development, and compensation of all types of personnel.

♦ Technology development: Technology development consists of a range of activities that can be broadly grouped into efforts to improve the product and the process.

♦ Procurement: Procurement refers to the function of purchasing inputs used in the firm's value chain, not to the purchased inputs themselves. The cost of procurement activities themselves usually represents a small, if not insignificant, portion of total costs but often has a large impact on the firm's overall cost and differentiation.

For those that do not identify with terms like inbound logistics, operations, outbound logistics, or firm infrastructure to represent their business processes, as an alternative, the value chain definition itself could be used to group activities into business processes. Using the value chain definition as a guide, the generic business processes of a service organization might be defined as design new services, procure materials and supplies, provide service, market service, deliver service, and provide customer support. Either way it is a tool to serve as a starting point. In the end, business processes must reflect the nomenclature and terminology of the specific business.

Another tool helpful in defining business processes and activities comes from Arthur Andersen and the International Benchmarking Clearinghouse (IBC). Founded in 1992 by the APQC and supported by almost 400 member organizations, the IBC is a leader in promoting, facilitating, and improving benchmarking. Arthur Andersen and the IBC have developed a process classification scheme to classify activities and business processes. The purpose of the process classification scheme is to enable the reliable collection and comparability of business process and activity data and information. This tool is particularly useful in situations where there is intent to use ABM to support benchmarking initiatives, because activities are classified in a way that make them comparable with the IBC member organizations and other organizations that use this tool.

An overview of the process classification scheme is set forth in Exhibit 5–1. In this schematic, business processes are classified as either operating processes or management and support processes. Operating processes, shown across the top, include understand markets and customers, develop vision and strategy, design products and services, market and sell, produce and deliver for either manufacturing or service organizations, and finally, invoice and service customers. Management and support processes are shown at the bottom of the schematic and include develop and manage human resources, manage information, manage financial and physical resources, execute environmental management program, manage external relationships, and manage improvement and change. Activities for each of the operating processes and management and support processes identified by Arthur Andersen and the IBC are set forth in Exhibits 5–2 and 5–3, respectively.

As an alternative to either of the above tools, simply obtaining business process relationship maps, complete with activity listings, from organizations that have completed this work will be enormously valuable. The more similar to the business being analyzed, the better. For some industries, activity and business process templates are available. Examples of business process relationship maps for a large multinational manufacturer of computers, an oil and gas producing company, an industrial distributor, and a medical supplier are set forth in Exhibits 5–4, 5–5, 5–6, and 5–7, respectively, and are described in the following.

The business process relationship map for a large computer manufacturer is presented in Exhibit 5–4. Operating business processes are grouped under the headings of opportunity/solution definition, solution building, and solution delivery. The operating business processes under opportunity/solution definition are market information capture, market selection, and identifying requirements. The business processes under solution building are hardware development, software development, services development, and production. Supporting business processes are shown at the bottom and include marketing, solution integration, finan-

Exhibit 5–1. Process Classification Scheme—An Overview

Operating Processes:

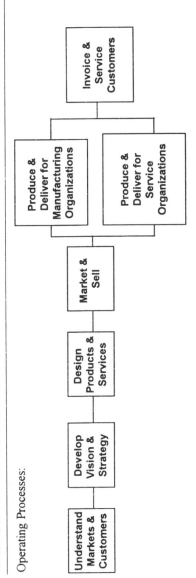

Management & Support Processes:

Develop & Manage Human Resources

Manage Information

Manage Financial & Physical Resources

Execute Environmental Management Program

Manage External Relationships

Manage Improvement & Change

Exhibit 5–2. Process Classification Scheme—Operating Processes

1. Understand Markets & Customers

1.1 Determine customer needs and wants
1.2 Measure customer satisfaction
1.3 Monitor changes in market or customer expectations

2. Develop Vision & Strategy

2.1 Monitor the external environment
2.2 Define the business concept and organizational strategy
2.3 Design the organizational structure and relationships between organizational units
2.4 Develop and set organizational goals

3. Design Products & Services

3.1 Develop new product/service concept and plans
3.2 Design, build, and evaluate prototype products or services
3.3 Refine existing products/services
3.4 Test effectiveness of new or revised products or services
3.5 Prepare for production
3.6 Manage the product/service development process

4. Market & Sell

4.1 Market products or services to relevant customer segments
4.2 Process customer orders

5. Produce & Deliver - *Manufacturing*

5.1 Plan for and acquire necessary resources or inputs
5.2 Convert resources or inputs into products
5.3 Make delivery
5.4 Manage produce and deliver process

6. Produce & Deliver - *Service*

6.1 Plan and acquire necessary resources
6.2 Develop human resource skills
6.3 Deliver service to the customer
6.4 Ensure quality of service

7. Invoice & Service Customer

7.1 Bill the customer
7.2 Provide after sales service
7.3 Respond to customer inquiries

Exhibit 5–3. Process Classification Scheme—Management & Support Process

8. Develop & Manage Human Resouces

8.1 Create human resource strategy
8.2 Ensure employee involvement
8.3 Train and educate employees
8.4 Recognize and reward employee performance
8.5 Ensure employee well-being and morale
8.6 Manage relocation of personnel

9. Manage Information

9.1 Manage information systems
9.2 Evaluate and audit information quality

10. Manage Financial & Physical Resources

10.1 Manage financial resources
10.2 Process financial and accounting transctions
10.3 Report information
10.4 Conduct internal audits
10.5 Manage the tax function
10.6 Manage physical resources

11. Execute Environmental Management Program

11.1 Formulate environmental management strategy
11.2 Ensure compliance with regulation
11.3 Train and educate employees
11.4 Implement pollution prevention program
11.5 Manage remediation efforts
11.6 Implement emergency response program
11.7 Manage government agency and public relations
11.8 Manage acquisition/divestiture environmental information system
11.9 Monitor environmental management program

12. Manage External Relationships

12.1 Communicate with shareholders
12.2 Manage government relationships
12.3 Build lender relationships
12.4 Develop public relations program
12.5 Interface with board of directors
12.6 Develop community relations
12.7 Manage legal and ethical issues

13. Manage Improvement & Change

13.1 Measure and monitor overall organization performance
13.2 Conduct quality assessment
13.3 Benchmark performance
13.4 Make process improvements
13.5 Manage change
13.6 Implement TQM

Exhibit 5-4. Business Process Relationship Map for a Multinational Computer Manufacturing Company

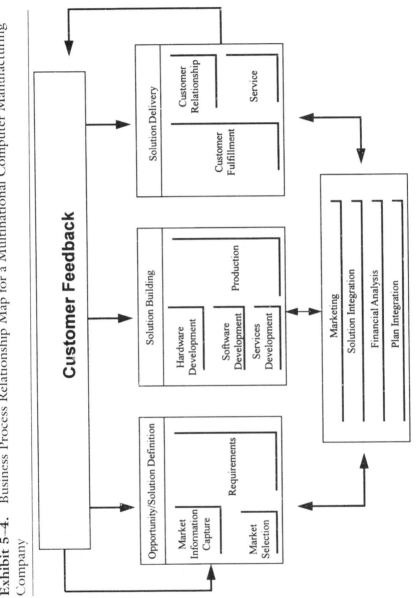

80

cial analysis, and plan integration. As illustrated at the top of the map, all business processes are directed and driven by customer feedback.

A business process relationship map for an oil- and natural gas–producing company is shown in Exhibit 5–5. The depicted organization is in the oil and gas production area only, so there are no business processes associated with the refining of crude oil or the delivery of natural gas, fuel oil, or gasoline to consumers. Business processes are captured under the broad categories of exploration and drilling, produce oil and gas, and sales and distribution. The business processes listed under each category were considered core or operating business processes. In addition to the 12 core business processes, 8 supporting business processes were identified.

Industrial distributors play a major role in supplying our schools, factories, hospitals, and service organizations. Because distributors do not have production processes, their business process relationship maps can be simplified. In this example, an industrial distributor of maintenance, repair items, and operating supplies defined their core operating business processes as order products, receive products, store products, take customer orders, pick orders, ship orders, bill customer, and recover from mistakes and problems. The business process relationship map is shown in Exhibit 5–6.

The supplier of test equipment to the medical industry might depict a business process relationship map as set forth in Exhibit 5–7. In this example, there are four core operating business processes of develop new products, sell products, make and deliver products, and perform service and repair calls. Supporting activities were grouped into two supporting business processes of train personnel and management planning, reporting, and control. For illustration, key activities that might be part of this business process relationship map are set forth in Exhibit 5–8.

Anyone with a little creativity and a basic understanding of their business ought to be able to initially define business processes and key activities without reference to the work done by others. Building a business process relationship map is helpful, especially for communication and big picture understanding. To be useful, the business process relationship map should address and reflect the consensus view of business processes in the organization. If you cannot get people to agree on business processes, it is doubtful that consensus could ever be reached on activities.

If the organization already has a business process relationship map, use it, if possible, and tie activities to it. If defining activities and linking to business processes has been difficult, then consider developing an overall

Exhibit 5–5. Business Process Relationship Map for an Oil- and Gas-Producing Company

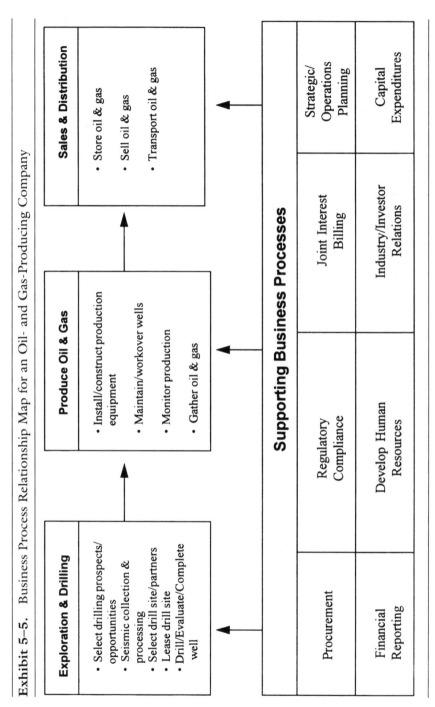

Exploration & Drilling

- Select drilling prospects/opportunities
- Seismic collection & processing
- Select drill site/partners
- Lease drill site
- Drill/Evaluate/Complete well

Produce Oil & Gas

- Install/construct production equipment
- Maintain/workover wells
- Monitor production
- Gather oil & gas

Sales & Distribution

- Store oil & gas
- Sell oil & gas
- Transport oil & gas

Supporting Business Processes

| Procurement | Regulatory Compliance | Joint Interest Billing | Strategic/ Operations Planning |
| Financial Reporting | Develop Human Resources | Industry/Investor Relations | Capital Expenditures |

Exhibit 5–6.   Business Process Relationship Map for an Industrial Distributor

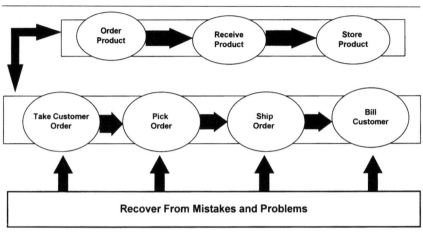

Exhibit 5–7.   Business Process Relationship Map for a Medical Company

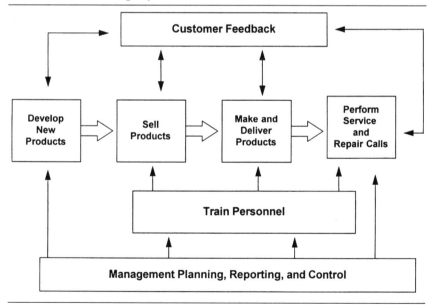

Exhibit 5–8. Medical Company Business Processes and Key Activities

Develop New Products

Develop prototypes

Test prototypes

Research market

Analyze cost

Sell Products

Prepare technical proposals

Attend trade shows and conventions

Make sales calls on hospitals

Make and Deliver Products

Assemble machines

Test and inspect

Box and ship

Assemble electrical component

Purchase material and supply

Schedule and inventory control (production control)

Perform Service and Repair Calls

Prepare written reports

On-site repair work

Train Personnel

Prepare training

Conduct classroom training

Administer training (scheduling, food, supplies, etc.)

Management Planning, Reporting, and Control

Prepare sales orders and billings

Prepare strategic plans and budgets

Prepare financial reports

Approve credit and collection

Administer employee benefits

business process relationship map and tie previously defined activities to it. If the organization is just getting started with ABM and business processes have never been defined, take the time to do it. Even if the initial ABM project is directed at only a fraction of the total business, the perspective of how the initial effort fits in the big picture will be valuable.

Bottom-up approach

Most ABM implementations utilize a bottom-up approach to defining business processes and activities. Specifying activities bottom-up means going to the department work level as the starting point. Activities are documented based on discussion, interviews, observation, and analysis. Once defined, activities are linked together through their inputs and outputs in a chain to represent a business process. The bottom-up approach produces a detailed picture of activities and a thorough understanding of activities at the task level. Ultimately, this detailed analysis is required in a top-down approach in order to validate, add, delete, change, and modify the initial definitions of business processes and activities. The problem with the bottom-up approach, absent a top-down look, is the tendency to define too many activities. Unless due care is exercised, the bottom-up approach can end up specifying thousands of activities.

Combining a top-down perspective with detailed analysis and data gathering at the department level will result in better definition and understanding of the key and significant activities. Specifying an activity as key and significant to the organization implies a willingness to measure and monitor the performance of that activity. Making that selection, without reference or consideration to the organization taken as a whole, is difficult. Activity definitions are enhanced and easier to understand when tied to business processes.

Criteria for Selecting/Stating Activities

As a general rule, the criteria for selection of activities is key and significant and relevant for decision making. Key and significant means those 20% of total activities that represent 80% of total costs. The primary criteria for stating an activity is to use a verb and a noun. Assemble component, drill hole, prepare report, set up machine, take customer order, conduct survey, receive raw material, and select vendors are examples of activities that have been defined with a verb and a noun. It is often necessary and helpful to insert an adjective between the verb and noun for further clarification. For example, the conduct survey activity might be enhanced to read conduct customer survey as a way to distinguish this activity from a conduct employee survey activity.

There are a number of specific criteria to consider when specifying an activity as key and significant:

1. **Where the company interacts with customers.** Key and significant should include those activities that external customers see and, from which, make judgment about the entire organization. As an example, customers of commercial airline carriers make judgments about the airline on the basis of activities they directly come in contact with, such as checking luggage, making reservations, or passenger check-in. To the airline passenger, activities that they have no contact with, such as pay vendor and prepare purchase orders, are not relevant. An airline can be the best in the world at the activity of preparing purchase orders, but it will not matter to the customer if the checking luggage activity is not done well.

2. **Activities that are high cost.** Activities that consume large amounts of resources or activities that drive other high-cost activities are key and significant. It is not unusual for the ten highest-cost activities to represent over one-third of total cost. For example, one company identified 14 business processes and 157 activities at the completion of their company-wide ABM implementation. The top ten activities accounted for 54% of total payroll-related costs. In applying this criteria use the *Willie Sutton rule,* which is to focus on the high-cost activities. The rule is named after bank robber Willie Sutton, who—when asked "why do you rob banks?"—is reputed to have replied "because that's where the money is."

3. **Activities that are core or sustaining.** The basic activities required to deliver the organization's products or services are key and significant.

4. **Activities that support objectives.** Strategic visions, missions, and goals are accomplished through activities. Work (activities) necessary to accomplish the goals must be performed and completed. Activities critical to meeting strategic missions, goals, and objectives are key and significant.

5. **Activities with potential for competitive advantage.** Any activity with potential to outperform competitors and provide competitive advantage should be considered as key and significant.

The specification and documentation of activities and business processes is critical to a successful ABM implementation. Failure to define and reach consensus on business processes and activities at the appropriate level of detail for relevance and decision making will create a cost driver to the ABM effort and reduce its ability to serve the organization.

DEFINE ACTIVITY OUTPUTS/MEASURES

Defining activity outputs/measures is important work that must be undertaken as part of the activity analysis. The work is important to a successful ABM implementation because many of the activity outputs and output measures will be used as activity drivers to trace activity costs to cost objects. In addition, defined and quantified activity outputs are necessary parts of basic productivity measures of activity performance. Finally, defining and quantifying activity outputs is important work to complete because the activity output is what the customer or user of an activity receives. Activity outputs are, in a sense, mini services and products. Customers and users of activities require only the activity output. Even a minimal level of customer or user satisfaction requires definition of what is being provided.

The word output is like the word process. It can mean different things to different people and is often overused. Webster's dictionary defines output as "Something that is put out or produced." Factories put out products, restaurants produce meals, mills put out flour, utilities produce energy, computers put out information to printers, and VCRs put out audio and video signals to television sets. Tasks, activities, business processes, and entire organizations each have outputs. The final output of all processes and activities performed by a company is its products and services. No wonder the word output is overworked. We use it in so many places for so many different things. With respect to defining outputs and measuring output quantity for an organization's key and significant activities, the objective is to identify and quantify what is accomplished or produced as a result of each activity. Activity outputs are whatever was produced, transformed, or completed by an activity.

Some activity outputs are easier to define and observe than others. Activities performed on a manufacturing floor are typically easy to see and therefore easy to define. We can watch an activity take place and observe the output. Activities performed by a tax department or activities performed in research and development areas are harder to define and observe. In the tax department, the output of an activity like research tax law might be difficult to define. The output might be researched tax question or interpretation of law. The output might be a position on a tax deduction. Despite the apparent difficulty, however, activity outputs for most activities can be defined.

Activity outputs can be quantified and measured. The most common activity output measures are simply the number of outputs performed or outputs completed. For example, the output measure for an activity drill hole might simply be the number of holes drilled. Where holes are drilled in different size or at differing depths, the number of holes drilled might not be an appropriate measure of output because some holes take longer to drill than others. In this case, the amount of metal or wood displaced by drilling might be a better measure of activity output. Activity outputs and measures are important because they enable the total cost of an activity to be related to work performed. Exhibit 5–9 provides examples of outputs and output measures for 18 activities.

Dividing the total activity cost by the output of that activity produces the cost of an individual activity output or cost per unit of activity output. While total activity costs are typically not comparable to other organizations, cost per unit of activity output often is. The reason for this, quite simply, is that while the total activity cost of two organizations could be the same, the resulting activity output in each of those organizations could be substantially different. The fact that they spend the same total amount on the same activity does not make them comparable. Only a cost per unit of activity output would be comparable.

For example, assume Organization A spends $1 million per year on its activity of taking customer orders. No one knows whether $1 million is good or bad or whether it should be more or less. The number itself cannot even be compared with that of other organizations unless volume and workloads are identical. However, the cost per unit of activity output can be compared. If Organization A's take customer order activity had an output of 100,000 customer orders, the unit price, or cost to take a customer order, would be $10.00. This per unit cost result could be compared with Organization B, which might only spend a total of $100,000 on its activity of take customer orders. If Organization B's output for this activity was 5,000 customer orders, then its cost per unit of activity output, or customer order, would be $20.00. Even though Organization A spends more total dollars on its activity, from a cost and productivity standpoint, it performs better than Organization B.

Exhibit 5–9. Activity Outputs and Measures

Activity	Activity Output	Measure(s) of Activity Output
Calibrate tools	A calibrated tool	Number of tools calibrated
Certify vendor	A certified supplier	The number of certified suppliers
Count inventory	A counted inventory item	The number of inventory items counted
Inspect raw materials	An inspected raw material	The number of raw materials inspected The number of inspections
Design a prototype	A prototype	Number of prototypes designed
Develop a bill of activity	A bill of activity	The number of bills of activities The number of activity sequences
Maintain routing	A revised set of routing instructions A revised production order	The number of routings The number of line items per routing The number of production orders changed
Select vendor	A selected supplier	The number of suppliers selected
Install new equipment	An installed piece of equipment	The number of pieces of equipment installed The number of steps in the installation process
Resolve legal issues	A resolved legal issue	The number of legal issues resolved

Exhibit 5–9. (*Continued*)

Activity	Activity Output	Measure(s) of Activity Output
Assemble components	An assembled component or subassembly	The number of components assembled The number of assembly line items
Expedite work order	An expedited work order	The number of work orders expedited The number of transactions expedited
Seal container	A sealed container	The number of containers sealed The number of seals
Setup Machine	A setup	Number of setups Number of equivalent setups
Ship finished goods	A shipped finished good	The number of shipments The number of finished goods shipped
Test sample	A tested sample	The number of samples tested The number of tests
Forecast sales	A sales forecast	The number of sales forecasts The number of line items per sales forecast
Issue checks	A check	The number of checks
	A cash transfer	The number of transfers

Absent the ability to compare a cost per unit of activity output with that of another organization, the information is still relevant and useful. The cost per unit of activity output represents a productivity measure an organization can use as a stake in the ground to represent current performance. Over time, the cost of an activity output can be tracked to determine whether progress is being made.

Surprisingly, many people (especially in support areas) have never thought of their job's activities as having an output. They struggle with defining activity outputs for the first time. Once documented and defined, people can begin to visualize the measurement of output. First, through output measures, we can quantify the amount of work completed. Later, through activity performance measures, we can quantify how well the work was performed.

IDENTIFYING THE CUSTOMER/USER OF ACTIVITY OUTPUTS

Activities have customers or users of its outputs. Customers can be internal or external. Internal customers of activity outputs can be other activities or other areas of the business. Examples of external customers, in addition to the consumer of the organization's products and services, include tax authorities, regulatory agencies, banks, and investors who use the information outputs associated with accounting and financial reporting activities.

For most activities, identifying customers/users of activity output is not difficult. Any difficulty encountered comes from those activities with multiple customers. For example, the pay employee activity would have state and federal payroll taxing authorities as customers in addition to the actual internal user of the paycheck, the employee. In these situations, it is helpful to determine the primary customer of the activity as a way to focus on the primary user.

Identifying the customer of an activity has enormous value. First, it helps to focus people toward producing activity outputs that meet customer requirements. In addition, the customer is instrumental in determining the value of an activity and should have the ultimate say in determining the performance criteria of an activity. Activities that produce output that no one uses are certainly nonvalue added and candidates for immediate elimination.

PERFORM VALUE-ADDED ANALYSIS

Some activities add value to products/services and organizational goals; other activities do not. Specifying an activity as value added or nonvalue added can evoke considerable discussion and debate in an organization. Part of the difficulty is that everyone seems to have a different view or definition of nonvalue added. Some people define value added as touch (direct) labor activities only, with all other activities deemed nonvalue added. Others interpret value added as what the customer is willing to pay for. Activities other than these are nonvalue added.

Another difficulty is the general inability for people to see their own work as nonvalue added. For example, a person that corrects data keying errors might view their job as value added and argue that by correcting errors, thousands of dollars might be saved, thus "creating value." An outside perspective might point out, correctly, that the activity of correcting errors is only done because something was not done right the first time and that to redo something is nonvalue added. Another example is rework performed on the manufacturing floor. To the person who reworks a part to save it from the scrap pile, these efforts would certainly be perceived as valuable, even heroic. Again, to the outsider, reworking a part because it was not done correctly the first time would not be value added.

As the previous definitions of value added and nonvalue added illustrated, through words like "an activity that is considered" and "reflects a belief," even the CAM-I cost management experts have difficulty defining the terms. People consider and believe in different things. What is important to the organization is to reach a consensus definition that everyone understands. Once reached, activities can be classified in accordance with the definition. Clarity and understanding between value and nonvalue added is achieved when people understand and accept the reasons why an activity is classified as nonvalue added or value added. No longer is it conceptual. The examples of non-value-added activities are real.

Most people perform their value-added analysis by simply designating an activity as value added or nonvalue added. It is one or the other. This level of analysis is insufficient because every value-added activity includes non-value-added tasks or steps. A more thorough analysis should be undertaken to identify the potential for improvement in value-added activities.

The categorization of activities as value added or nonvalue added is important and useful because it influences the type of improvement initiative that works best. In the case of a value-added activity, improvement initiatives would be directed toward streamlining, improving what is being done, and optimizing performance. In the case of a non-value-added activity, improvement initiatives would be directed toward eliminating or minimizing the activity (we're not trying to do it better; we're trying to quit doing it all together).

IDENTIFY COST DRIVERS

Cost drivers identify the cause of activity cost and are valuable because they point people to take action at the root cause level. All activities have multiple cost drivers, some of which are controllable and some of which are not. *Cost driver analysis* is defined as the examination, quantification, and explanation of the effects of cost drivers. Management often uses the results of cost driver analyses in continuous improvement programs to help reduce throughput time, improve quality, and reduce cost. The objective in cost driver analysis is to identify as many cost drivers as possible and then prioritize for action based on the organization's ability to influence the driver.

As defined by CAM-I, a cost driver is any factor that causes a change in the cost of an activity. Any factor includes almost anything under the sun. Weather can be a cost driver, a cause of cost, to the trucking industry at times during the winter. An organization's own policies can be cost drivers. For example, federal government procurement policy and public law that require multiple and often excessive requests for quotations (RFQs) can result in hundreds of responses, all of which must be reviewed as part of procuring a product or service. Employee turnover, inadequately trained personnel, antiquated/outdated equipment, and complexity of product/services might all be factors that cause cost.

In addition, activities can be cost drivers of other activities. For example, the activity of select vendors might be a cost driver on manufacturing activities because poor selection of vendors might result in poor quality or late delivered parts. Poor quality and unanticipated delays are frequently cited cost drivers. Product/service design activities can be cost drivers, when multiple or custom parts are used rather than standard parts.

The value of identifying cost drivers for each activity is to direct improvement efforts to the cause of cost and avoid treating the symptom. It does not do much good to focus an improvement initiative on teaching people to respond quickly to product leaks if the cause of the work is an inadequately designed seal. Conversely, it will not do much good to eliminate a cost driver if that driver is not truly the cause of cost. A thorough cost driver analysis must be performed to get to the root cause.

Cost drivers can be broadly divided into external and internal cost drivers. External cost drivers are outside the organization and typically cannot be influenced in the short term. Regulatory requirements, economic events, and supply disruptions all could be cost drivers and not controlled or influenced in the short term. Internal cost drivers are inside the organization and can be generally influenced in the short to medium term. Often, cost driver analysis identifies drivers that effect multiple activities. They seem to show up everywhere. These are the cost drivers to attack first because the impact is so great. Eliminating one cost driver improves many activities.

DETERMINE ACTIVITY PERFORMANCE AND GOALS

Activity output measures provide information about how much work was completed. Activity performance measures are designed to provide information on how well the activity work was performed. There are four elements of activity performance: productivity, quality, cycle time, and customer satisfaction. In isolation, none of them can fully measure activity performance. To judge total activity performance, each of the elements must be considered jointly.

Productivity

Productivity is a measure of efficiency and is calculated by dividing the resources consumed by an activity (inputs) by the output of the activity. Estimating and monitoring productivity are among the most critical information outputs that management can use to judge performance. Resources (inputs) can be expressed in time or monitory terms. Productivity improves when we produce more with less, produce more with the same, or produce the same with less. When expressed in monitory terms, productivity improves when the cost per unit of output declines. This productivity calculation links the physical output of an activity to its cost. Productivity can be calculated at the business process, activity, or task levels.

Quality

Quality has many meanings for many people. In judging quality performance of an activity, it simply means conformance to specification. Quality is perhaps the clearest example of why the four elements of activity performance must be analyzed in tandem. Poor conformance to specifications directly affects productivity. The same nonconformance also lengthens cycle time. And quality as a performance measurement is one of the most useful information outputs for management to achieve its goal of providing the lowest product/service cost while at the same time meeting customer needs.

Cycle Time

Cycle time is a measurement of the total elapsed time it takes to complete an activity or a business process. The total cycle time to make a product or service and deliver it to the customer is the summation of the "nonoverlapped" cycle time for each of the activities necessary to produce and deliver a product or service to customers. Cycle time may be expressed in hours, days, weeks, months, or years. Like the other performance measurements, reduced cycle time is predicated on improved productivity, increased quality, and customer satisfaction. Cycle time measures are best applied at the business process level, where the integration of activities is critical to reducing cycle times. Rarely is it effective to reduce the cycle time of a single activity when the real opportunity is to compress multiple activities.

Customer Satisfaction

Improved productivity, increased quality, and reduced cycle time are meaningless if customers are dissatisfied. As a key performance measurement, customer satisfaction should be quantified and expressed at its source by the customer. For example, overall customer satisfaction for a given activity might be expressed on a scale of 1 to 5, where 1 is poor and 5 is excellent.

Unfortunately, initial measurements of activity performance provide little value. For example, knowing that the actual quality performance of the activity pay vendor invoices was ten errors per thousand or that the activity cost is $36.24 to pay each vendor invoice (productivity measure) does not tell us whether that is good or bad . . . it is what it is. But it is at least a starting point. By recording measures over time, a record of performance and rate of improvement can be established.

The problem with many performance measurement systems today is that they are inwardly focused. They compare ourselves with ourselves over time. Internal-based measures of performance do not tell people whether the improvements are good enough and from what level the improvements are coming. Five percent better than poor is still poor; 1% better than excellent is still more excellent. A 10% improvement of a key activity is not enough when competitors improve 20%. To effectively judge the performance of business processes and activities, managers need to compare, or benchmark, performance with the outside world.

Benchmarking, or *best practices,* is defined as a methodology that identifies an activity as the benchmark by which a similar activity will be judged. This methodology is used to assist in identifying a process or technique that can increase the effectiveness or efficiency of an activity. The source may be internal (e.g., taken from another part of the company) or external (e.g., taken from a competitor).

While, as noted, the foregoing performance measurements are interdependent, their relative ranking in importance is dependent upon a number of considerations, such as the specific activity, the type of product or service, the kind of organization, the industry, and the customer. If you believe the old axiom, you get what you measure, many of us who may still be providing performance measurements derived from historical cost-based standards, methods, and procedures will not drive a change in mind set toward continuous improvement. The key mix of measurements for success today must be derived from productivity, quality, cycle time, and customer satisfaction. Keep the following thoughts in mind when developing activity-based performance measures:

- If it seems obvious or intuitive, it's probably a good candidate for measurement.
- Performances measures should be simple (i.e., easy to communicate and understand) but not simplistic.
- Try it; test it; keep or discard it.
- Be visual and in graphical form.
- Select performance measures that focus on driving the right types of behavior.
- Link measures to objectives and strategies.
- Size or volume measures are not helpful by themselves.
- Measures should show relationships and ratios between variables.
- Experiment and improve over time.
- Do not measure unimportant or trivial items.
- Performance data should be easy and cost-effective to collect.

DEFINE OTHER ACTIVITY ATTRIBUTES

Many organizations find it useful to identify and define the attributes of an activity. *Attributes* are characteristics of activities, such as cost drivers and performance measures. *Activity attributes* are characteristics of individual activities. Attributes include cost drivers, cycle time, capacity, and performance measures. For example, a measure of the elapsed time required to complete an activity is an attribute.

Value-added or non-value-added, cost drivers, and activity performance measures are characteristics of activities and therefore attributes. These are important attributes covered previously. Other activity attributes include the following:

Primary Versus Secondary Activities

Primary activities represent the main activities of a department or organization. Secondary activities support primary activities. Many organizations designate activities as primary or secondary as a way to develop primary/secondary ratios. It is not unusual to find organizations that spend only 60% of their cost resources on primary activities and spend the remainder on activities of support. A target ratio for many companies is 80/20.

Core, Sustaining, and Discretionary

Core activities are those activities absolutely required to make or deliver a product or service to customers. *Sustaining activity* is defined as an activity that benefits an organization at some level (e.g., the company as a whole or a division, plant, or department) but not any specific cost object. Examples of such activities are preparation of financial statements, plant managers, and the support of community programs. Discretionary activities are important but not necessary, at least in the short term. Designating activities as core, sustaining, or discretionary often provides insight useful for decision making.

Strategic

Activities can be identified with the attribute strategic in order to place emphasis on them. In addition, the attribute strategic will enable the reporting of actual activity spending in activities required to achieve strategic missions and goals.

GATHER ACTIVITY DATA REQUIRED FOR ACTIVITY/PRODUCT COSTING

An important part of the activity analysis work is to gather data and information required to trace resource costs to activities and activity costs to cost objects. To determine activity cost, as a minimum, the percentage of people's time spent on the various activities must be documented. The facilities used and equipment required to perform an activity must be known. To determine product cost or other cost object, activity outputs or their activity drivers must be quantified, and a determination must be made as to the product, service, or other cost object that actually used the output.

The data and information requirements for activity/product costing were outlined and documented in Chapter 4. This data and information can be collected at many points in the activity analysis. On one extreme the activity analysis could be entirely completed before the first piece of information required for cost tracing was collected. Conversely, the accumulation of data needed to trace resources to activities could start immediately after activities were specified. More often than not, data will be gathered at several different points in the activity analysis.

6

Data Gathering

Garbage in, garbage out.

The quality and integrity of activity-based data affect the quality and integrity of the conclusions reached and recommendations made based on the analysis of that data. Taking action and making better decisions based on information and knowledge gained are what makes the ABM system valuable to the organization. Actions and decisions taken on incomplete, inaccurate, inadequate, or even misleading activity-based data and information could be disastrous. In addition, all ABM implementation efforts would be wasted if managers and decision makers believe the data are suspect and, therefore, take no actions. For these reasons, data gathering is a critical element to a successful ABM implementation.

There are a number of ways to collect and use data. One-on-one interviews with managers and employees are the most common and most overused methods. These one-on-one interviews are typically conducted with a representative sample of people (5 to 15% of total employees) to define activities, cost drivers, performance measures, resource drivers and activity drivers and for value analysis. Although in certain situations interviews are the preferred method of gathering data, in many situations this technique alone is inadequate. Experienced ABM implementors recognize the value and limitations of using observation, questionnaires, historical records and documents, and experts as additional sources of activity-based data and information.

99

The first half of this chapter will identify the various data collection techniques available to the ABM implementor and will discuss the major advantages and disadvantages of each. Most ABM implementations will employ a combination of techniques suited in the specific need and situation. Interviews are an important element for collecting data from the organization and will be used, in some form or other, in most ABM implementations. Therefore, the last half of this chapter will address this topic specifically, including interviewer competencies, interviewing avoids, and how to get started.

DATA COLLECTION TECHNIQUES

The primary data collection techniques available to the ABM implementor include interviews with department heads, interviews with departmental personnel, questionnaires, analysis of historical records and documents, panel of experts, observation, and group-based collection techniques. Each are reviewed and discussed in turn.

Interviews with Department Heads

The application of this technique typically takes the form of a one- or two-hour meeting between a member(s) of the ABM implementation team and the department manager. Collecting data at this level of the organization is effective early in an ABM implementation where the intent is an overview of departmental activities, including outputs and measures, cost drivers, existing departmental performance measures, and preliminary information on how resources are consumed in performing activities (manager's best guesses and estimates). To prove useful, these data must be supplemented with more rigorous analysis. Unless additional techniques are used, these interviews merely document the department activities from the manager's perspective. Another drawback with this method, if applied solely, is the lack of ownership, except by the manager, in the final result. The people who know the most about the work are not involved and lack ownership.

Another reason this technique is valuable in the early stages of implementation is because of the personal contact with managers. Early on, interviews provide a vehicle to transfer ABM knowledge to the manager and to address questions or concerns about the use, application, and value of activity-based information. Especially in small or specialized departments, the information provided by department managers is often completely adequate for the ABM implementation, and additional work might not be required.

This technique is very effective when performing the overall assessment of the applicability of ABM to the organization and in developing the initial implementation plan. Simple comparisons of traditional department cost information with ABM information, prepared on the basis of manager perspective, can be used to assess the applicability and usefulness of ABM information. In addition, these high-level interviews will help determine and prioritize the activity-based information that is most important to the managers.

Major advantages and disadvantages of this technique are summarized as follows:

Major Advantages

♦ Personal contact with management.

♦ Provides adequate preliminary information on activities, resource allocation, activity outputs, performance measures, and key issues.

Major Disadvantages

♦ Needs to be supplemented by other techniques, as interviews may be short and cover many topics.

♦ Does not involve people who do the work.

♦ Managers perspective only and may not reflect reality.

Interviews with Departmental Personnel

In the typical application of this technique a sample of departmental staff members are selected for more detailed interviews. For this technique to be successful the sample must be representative of the people who actually perform the work in the department and are knowledgeable about its performance. Interviews can be conducted on a one-on-one or two-on-two basis. These interviews are more detailed than interviews with managers and strive for a higher level of understanding. This level of interview drives understanding of activities to the task level and provides more accurate estimates of how people spend their time and how other resources are consumed by activities. These levels of interviews should be sufficient to develop clear definitions of activities.

Depending on the competence of the person doing the interview, opportunities for improvement and improvement ideas are easily identified.

The main drawback to this technique is the disruption of day-to-day operations. In addition, the one-on-one or two-on-two interview format is not particularly conductive to creativity.

The major advantages and disadvantages of this technique are as follows:

Major Advantages
♦ Provides better information on tasks.

♦ May identify additional problems and improvement ideas.

♦ Possibility of observation.

Major Disadvantages
♦ May disturb day-to-day business.

♦ Not conductive to creativity.

Questionnaires

Questionnaires are the least expensive method for collecting activity-based data and information. Used in areas where it can be effective, questionnaires are an easy and fast way to collect data. Questionnaires work best for collecting information from managerial and administrative employees. They do not work as well for line people. Perhaps it is because administrative and manager level employees are accustomed to filling out paper work and completing questionnaires. Most of the time they have a work area where they can sit down to complete the questionnaire. That is not always true for frontline operating personnel.

Questionnaires are effective only when properly designed and when people are properly prepared and trained to answer the questions or provide the information. For example, a questionnaire might ask a person to list activities and provide an estimate of time spent on each activity. If people do not understand the level at which information is being collected, the list might include 25 or more activities, which is not particularly useful. Or a questionnaire that asks the respondent to identify an activity as value added or nonvalue added would not be effective if the respondent was unclear as to the terms themselves. For most ABM implementations the primary use of questionnaires is in the collection of data on how people spend their time and on activity output information.

Because there is no personal contact with a questionnaire, the likelihood of identifying opportunities for improvement, political issues, and problems is limited. In addition, even the best of designed questionnaires often require clarification and follow-up to achieve understanding.

Major advantages and disadvantages of this technique are summarized as follows:

Major Advantages
♦ Inexpensive method of gathering information.

♦ Short elapsed time for collection of information.

♦ Most successful when used by managerial and administrative employees.

Major Disadvantages
♦ No personal contact.

♦ Political and personal issues and problems might not be identified.

♦ Clarification/follow-up often required to complement responses.

♦ Subject to misinterpretation and not always reliable.

Analysis of Historical Records, Reports, and Documents

Analysis of historical records, reports, and documents is probably the most underused data collection method and, in many situations, the most valuable. Especially in large organizations, there is a vast treasure chest of data and information contained in studies, brochures, 10-K fillings, internal financial reports, published articles, and desk drawers of managers. The 10-K and other filings with the Security Exchange Commission and annual reports to shareholders often describe the operations of public companies and are excellent source data for defining business processes and activities.

People are hired to do work (activities). Especially in large organizations, people are often assigned a job code or job classification that corresponds to a job description. Job codes and job descriptions are excellent source data for defining activities. Internal labor reporting systems, where payroll costs are collected by job code or job classification, can be an excellent source of data for tracing salary and wage costs to activities. This is especially true in situations where people tend to do just one or two activities. Large groups of people who are included in the same job code and who do the same activity simplifies cost tracing.

Internal studies, flowcharts, reports, and even documented procedures are all excellent sources of data that can provide insight to activities, cost drivers, performance measures, value-added analysis, and data required for tracing costs. The main problem encountered with these documents is that they are not always reliable or up-to-date. However, except in the extreme situations, documents that are not up-to-date still contain salvageable data and information. The effort to review and analyze historical records and documents is generally worthwhile.

The major advantages and disadvantages of this data collection technique are as follows:

Major Advantages
♦ Limited involvement of people to collect the information.

♦ Provides adequate information.

♦ Inexpensive.

♦ Enables building on an existing base of information.

Major Disadvantages
♦ Not always up-to-date.

♦ No personal contact.

♦ Key issues and problems may remain hidden.

Panel of Experts

A panel of experts is a group of knowledgeable people assigned to provide and document information or data about a specific aspect of the ABM implementation. Typically conducted in a workshop setting and led by a qualified facilitator, individual expertise and group creativity are combined to maximize the activity-based knowledge about a specific aspect of the business. A panel of experts could be formed to define the activities of a particular department. A panel of experts could be formed to develop a list of cost drivers or to develop a definition for a non-value-added activity. A facilitated workshop of department managers designed to identify, on a preliminary basis, business processes and key activities for an entire organization is another example of the use of a panel of experts.

The panel of experts technique must be used sparingly because it is time-consuming to the experts who attend. Depending on the workshop scope, as many as two days may be required. As a minimum, to be effective, workshops require one-half day. Additionally, facilitators outside the organization may be necessary.

Major advantages and disadvantages of this technique are summarized as follows:

Major Advantages
♦ Takes advantage of broad expertise.

♦ Helps create consensus.

Major Disadvantages
♦ Only effective in specific areas.

♦ Time-consuming.

Analysis of Diaries, Time Sheets, Logs, and Check Sheets

For organizations that require employees to keep track of their time, an analysis of diaries, time sheets, and time logs is generally sufficient to provide information on the percentage of time spent on activities and to help define activities. This analysis can be very time-consuming, especially when records are exceedingly detailed or illegible. However, if accurately kept, these records will provide the most accurate resource driver to trace salaries and wage costs to activities.

If the organization does not have an existing employee time reporting system, then one should not be put in to accommodate the ABM implementation, especially in the early stages, because most people do not like to record their time. If time keeping is perceived as a requirement of the ABM system, then people may view ABM as a labor reporting system and entirely miss the real benefits. Besides, ABM is only successful when people use the information. Efforts to implement labor reporting as a way to increase the accuracy of the information is pointless if no one finds value in the information to begin with. Let the users of activity-based information initiate recommendations and efforts to implement those labor-reporting systems required to capture activity data at the source.

One variation to a detailed labor reporting system might prove helpful when used with other techniques. Data must be gathered on how people spend their time. Interviews and questionnaires designed to gather this information simply ask the person, on the spot, and record the answer. How people actually spend their time can be significantly different than how they perceive it spent. Asking people to record their time, via a time sheet or log, by activity for a short period of time prior to the collection of data will result in more accurate information.

The major advantages and disadvantages of this technique are as follows:

Major Advantages
- ◆ Helps to identify activities.
- ◆ Percentage of time spent on each activity can easily be identified.
- ◆ Accurate for tracing people cost to activities.

Major Disadvantages
- ◆ Time-consuming.
- ◆ Can result in perception that ABM is a labor reporting system.

Observation

Observation is one of the least used data collection techniques. Much can be learned from open eyes and from observation. Short or repetitive activities, together with the tasks required to perform the activity, can be observed. Non-value-added activities that represent rework and correction can be seen. Major cost drivers like facility layout and production bottle necks can be obvious. Observation goes a long way toward understanding the flow of activities and business processes, especially if material flow or information flow is visible. The only real disadvantage is its limited application, because much of what goes on in organizations is not visible.

Major advantages and the disadvantage of this technique is summarized as follows:

Major Advantages
- ◆ Suitable for short, repetitive, and visible activities and processes.
- ◆ Facilitates understanding of business processes if material on information flow is visible.
- ◆ Accurate information on activity/tasks.

Major Disadvantage
- ◆ Limited application.

Group-Based Techniques

To facilitate consensus and ownership of data and information collected, many ABM implementors use group-based collection techniques. One of these techniques, the storyboard, was originated by Walt Disney in 1928 while working out of a garage on a cartoon entitled *Steamboat Willie*— the first talking cartoon.

Animating *Steamboat Willie* required thousands of drawings, and it was hard to know what had been finished and what still needed to be done. Drawings were piled in stacks all over the place. To regain control, Walt had the artists pin up drawings in sequence so that the pictures told the story. This storyboard quickly became a routine of the Walt Disney Studio's planning procedure and was very popular. Walt had always wanted involvement, and with the storyboard, everything was out in the open. Drawings were organized so that the creative team could see the entire cartoon plot in front of them. If scenes were eliminated, they could be unpinned and discarded. Walt could walk in at any time of the day or night and see progress at a glance. Storyboards keep branching out into many uses. In fact, Disneyland and Walt Disney World were operationally planned using storyboards.

Storyboarding and similar group-based collection techniques involve the collection of activity-based information and data in this same visible way, using involvement, teaming, and creativity. With group-based techniques, teams are established at the department level and through structured and often facilitated work sessions, activities and processes are documented on walls with symbols that can be easily moved and replaced. Department personnel are encouraged to view the documentation of activities, flow charts, cost drivers, and value-added analysis as the work progresses and to add their comments, suggestions, and observations. Data on how people spend their time by activity is often accomplished by the assignment of time directly to the posted flowcharts.

Two very successful group-based techniques are Rapid Vision and FastTrack ABM. Rapid Vision, developed by Arthur Andersen, collects activity information while simultaneously obtaining employee buy-in and validating the information. This communication tool allows groups to structure their thinking by providing a visual depiction of ideas which in turn become physical objects (cards) that group members reorganize to streamline data collection. FastTrack ABM, jointly developed by Michael Roberts and myself, is unique in its use of activity mapping and activity costing in a one-week fast-paced workshop. During the week, the team defines services and products, analyzes activities, develops activity maps, uses ABC techniques, identifies and prioritizes process improvement opportunities, and develops performance measures.

Group-based collection techniques are designed to move companies quickly from analysis to action. Workshops emphasize learning by doing. Workshop participants use actual operational data to analyze activities and processes within their own organization. Often, facilitators/instructors guide the team through the process of implementing ABM. The hands-on learning approach of group-based techniques provide an enhanced understanding of ABM and a feeling of accomplishment when the workshops are completed. Group-based techniques stimulate creativity, build organizational consensus, and generate improvement process innovation.

Major advantages and disadvantages of group-based collection techniques include the following:

Major Advantages
♦ Consensus, ownership, and buy-in.
♦ Information gained is immediately actionable.

Major Disadvantages
♦ Time-consuming, expensive.
♦ Disruptive to day-to-day operations.

All of the data collection techniques described can be used on an ABM implementation, and all have value. The selection and application of data collection techniques will vary from organization to organization and are situation specific. All techniques have been used with varying degrees of success. Some implementations rely exclusively on interviews; others rely exclusively on group involvement. Most ABM implementors mix, match, and adopt the techniques to their specific requirements and available resources.

INTERVIEWS

Interviews are an important part of data gathering and represent a significant portion of the resources consumed in the ABM implementation effort. A decision to interview a person is a minimum commitment of eight hours work. Just the meeting time to conduct a simple one-on-one interview often takes two hours; with two people involved in the interview it takes four hours total. Then there is documentation and follow-up. As a minimum, it will be necessary to furnish the person interviewed with a copy of the work documentation for comment and approval. Follow-up may be required for clarification and understanding. The commitment to these resources must be done intelligently.

Interviews are most often used to collect activity-based information and data for a department, section, or branch of an organization. One reason for this is that departments, sections, or branches represent a division of the total business structure into manageable parts. Each department represents a portion of the organization's cost structure and a distinct group of activities. In addition, each department includes knowledgeable people who understand the activities being performed and have a vested interest in their improvement. This predefined structure provides a logical framework for conducting interviews.

For interviews to be successful, they cannot be approached in a haphazard way. Too much of the ABM implementation resource is at risk. To use these resources intelligently, adequate preparation for the interview is required. Interviews must be conducted in a professional and competent manner. Pitfalls must be avoided; it is critical to get started on the right foot. A discussion of each of these areas—preparation and conducting interviews, interviewer competencies, interviewing pitfalls to avoid, and getting started—follows.

Preparation and Conducting Interviews

Selection of the person(s) to be interviewed and preparation for the interview(s) are two critical components to using interviewing techniques successfully. Selection and preparation, if inadequately done, are cost drivers to the ABM implementation. Selecting the wrong people to interview means additional interviews may be required. Lack of preparation may mean going back to collect information and data missed in the interview. Selection of who to interview is dependent on the requirements. In some cases it might be an in-house expert, a cross section of employees, managers only, or a combination of all three. Once determined, the success of the interview will be largely dependent on preparation.

As a minimum, the interviewee must have as much pertinent information as possible before being interviewed. A letter outlining objectives and procedures should be sent to each person or group of people to be interviewed ahead of time. The letter should contain the specified number of hours (allow two hours) for the interview, an article explaining what ABM is, and an interview agenda. Interview agendas will vary depending on whom is being interviewed and what information and data is required.

An example of an interview agenda with a department manager where the objective is to gain an understanding of key and significant activities of the department might include the following items for discussion:

1. Purpose and rationale.
2. The managers questions regarding the use and application of ABM.
3. The major time- and resource-consuming activities of the department.
4. The output, product, or service resulting from each activity.
5. The percentage of people resources each activity consumes (accounting for 100%).
6. Any factors that cause these activities to fluctuate (cost drivers).

As a practical matter, it is often difficult to collect all the activity-based information and data required in a single interview at one time. Therefore, many implementors find it easier to collect data in two interviews, the first of which is directed toward defining activities, outputs, and time percentages. The second interview, conducted a week or two later, collects the remainder of the activity-based information.

It is a good idea to use a standard worksheet to collect activity-based data. This is especially true when multiple teams or individuals are conducting the interviews. First, the use of a standard form ensures that all the necessary information has been collected. In addition, consolidating, analyzing, and using the data is simplified when accumulated in a standard format. Finally, the form provides a simple way for the interviewee(s) to sign off on the data collected. An example of a standard evaluation worksheet for both the first and second interview is set forth in Exhibits 6–1 and 6–2, respectively.

Building the activity evaluation worksheet into a database application software program like Microsoft's Access is very helpful. In addition to the obvious benefit of eliminating paper and ease of data movement, analysis is simplified and easily accessible when preparing the activity dictionary. In a network environment it also enables the interviewee to review the data and make changes on-line, thus minimizing follow-up efforts.

An excellent technique for conducting interviews is to use flip charts to record the information gathered in the interview. Most people who conduct interviews do so by sitting across from the person being interviewed, recording responses to questions on $8\frac{1}{2} \times 11$ tablets. While this works fine for supervisory, manager, and executive level personnel, many people, especially those unaccustomed to being interviewed, find this method

Exhibit 6–1. Activity Evaluation Worksheet (Page 1)

Department _____   Person Interviewed _____

Date _____   Interviewer _____

Activity	Activity Description	Activity Output	Activity Output Measures	Time %	Notes
1.					
2.					
3.					
4.					
5.					
6.					
N.					

uncomfortable and even threatening. Because they cannot see what is being recorded, they turn timid and tight lipped.

Recording responses on flip charts takes the mystery away. Everything is visible, making changes and adding or deleting items easy. The person(s) being interviewed can see what is being recorded. This is less threatening and more conducive to creativity. Using flip charts has an additional benefit of enabling the person to sign-off on the interview notes. In essence they can approve what is been recorded, thus reducing some of the follow-up that might otherwise be required. When using the recommended flip chart technique, the data recorded on the flip chart can be entered into the activity evaluation worksheet by either the interviewee or interviewer.

Interviewer Competencies

Some people do a better job of interviewing people for the purpose of gathering data than others. Interviewer competence can be expressed in

Exhibit 6–2.   Activity Evaluation Worksheet (Page 2)

Department _____   Person Interviewed _____

Date _____   Interviewer _____

Activity	VA/NVA	Performance Measures	Cost Drivers	Customer of Output	Other Activity Attributes	Notes
1.						
2.						
3.						
4.						
5.						
6.						
N.						

terms of technical competence and personal competence. Technical competencies include the following:

◆ Understanding the business environment. Organizational structure (for the whole company), functional and departmental structure, and company strategy, vision, and direction must be understood. People that possess this competency have an excellent grasp of the total business.

◆ Understanding the key business processes. An individual with this competency has the ability to think about the business horizontally across departmental boundaries.

◆ Understanding the interviewee's specific situation. This includes understanding the size (volume), growth (steady or shrinking), recent changes in operations, supplier of input, and customer of output.

◆ System smarts. A person with this competency knows how to get things done quickly within the system and, if necessary, outside the system.

Personal competencies include the following:

◆ Ability to gain support. Some people are born with the ability to gain support and to work in a team environment. Others have to develop these abilities. The ability to gain support is a personal competency that will allow people to share knowledge and opinion more openly and freely.

◆ Translator or interpreter versus an auditor. There are two ways of asking the same question, for example: What other activities do you perform? and Is that all you do? They carry a completely different tone. Interviews are successful when relevant and factual data and information is gathered. People do not like to share information with someone perceived as checking up or watching over them.

◆ Improvement orientation versus problem identification orientation. This is a mind-set. Some people are oriented toward improvement, others toward problem identification. Interviews that are oriented toward improvement are more rewarding. Interviews oriented toward problem identification can end up as griping sessions.

◆ Integrity. Information and data given in confidence and trust must remain as such.

◆ Listener/Learner. People will share information best with an active listener and learner. A good interviewer spends most of the time listening, not talking.

◆ Flexible. Interviewer should be flexible about schedules and preconceived notions.

Interviewing Pitfalls to Avoid

Pitfalls to watch out for during an interview include avoiding a courtroom atmosphere. The interview is a conversation, not a trial. Remember that nothing is cast in concrete; things can be modified, added, or deleted later. No final judgments should be made in the interview. This carries over to include avoiding final hard copy analysis prematurely. Let the interviewee review a draft copy of the interview, and rework it if necessary. Throughout the interview, avoid putting the interviewee on the defensive. For example, do not push when you get a "don't know" reply. Don't dig too deep, too fast. The interviewee should send you comfort level signals.

Getting Started

Interviews are successful when the person understands, in advance, the rationale for ABM, the objectives of the interview, the procedure to be followed, and finally, what will happen after the interview. This can be done in writing before the interview or simply done verbally at the time the interview takes place. Starting correctly is important.

Getting started correctly was critical to the Defense Logistics Agency (DLA), a major agency of the Department of Defense, whose ABM implementation effort involved interviews with thousands of people. Most of these interviews were performed at the branch/section level of the agency, which is equivalent to departments/subdepartments in commercial organizations. The rationale, objectives, procedures, and next steps used by the interviewers to kick off and guide the interview might have sounded like the following to those attending the interview.

Rationale

As you may know, the DLA has initiated a program being adopted across all DLA units, to better manage our activities and our costs. The program is called activity-based costing and is supportive of the new administration's focus on "creating a government that works better and costs less."

Objectives

The objective of our interview is to identify and validate the major activities that people do in their jobs and then determine how much time is spent on each of those activities. We also want to get your ideas on a few additional points, such as:

1. What is the output of the activity?
2. Who is the customer or user of the activity?
3. What performance measures can be used to determine when an activity is being done well?
4. What causes the activity to cost more than it should or could (cost drivers)?

Procedures

We intend to make this interview as uncomplicated as possible for you. Much work has already been done within the DLA to identify key and significant activities. We want you to help us verify and validate the work that has already been done. We also want you to identify any key activities that are a part of your specific job but that we have not already captured. After this, we will ask you for estimates and ideas on the following:

1. The percentage of time typically spent on the activity.
2. The output of the activity: What does it produce?
3. The customer of the activity: Who gets the output?
4. Ways to measure the performance of activities.
5. Cost drivers or the cause of activity cost.

We will gather your information on a flip chart pad so that it is clear to you what we are writing down. This will be your information, not our interpretation. You can change anything at any time, so do not feel you have to be absolutely correct before saying anything. This is a live document.

Now let us identify the activities you do in your job. (The interviewer had a choice of methods to define activities. First, show the list of activities, and ask them to identify which ones they do. Or ask them to describe what they do, and later match, or add, what the individual says to the master list of activities.) Do these activities account for 90% (or more) of what you do? Is there any key or significant activity we need to add?

The next procedure is to determine the estimated percentage of your time spent on each activity. Which activity takes up the most time? Which activity takes the least amount of time? How would you rank the activities in terms of time spent (1, 2, 3, etc.)? For the activity marked as number 1 (or the most time), what percentage of your time is spent on it? We will then proceed through the other activities to get your percentages for each activity you have identified.

Now that we have identified your activities and the percentages of your time spent on each one, we want your ideas about these activities. Beginning with the highest activity, or most time spent:

1. What is the output?
2. Who is the customer?

3. What performance measure or criteria could be used to determine whether this activity is being done well?

4. What are some cost drivers that drive the cost of activity up?

We will proceed through the other activities (from the second most time spent through the least time spent) so that we capture all your ideas. Once completed, our interview is over.

Next steps

If you think of something to add or change over the next few days, give us a call. Within three days, we'll give you a hard copy of this chart pad. It will be on $8\frac{1}{2} \times 11$ paper. You will have an opportunity to review and approve what is written. In the meantime, we may need to contact you for clarification on some item. Please continue thinking about potential ways to improve any of these activities we have discussed today. Thanks for your help and participation in this effort.

Summary

Interviews with people at all levels of the organization, properly designed questionnaires, analysis of historical records and documents, using experts, and involving people with group-based techniques are all valuable for gathering data. Each has advantages in different situations. Correctly matching the technique to the situation will produce the best result.

Interviews remain an important source for gathering data and the primary vehicle for transferring specific ABM information. To be effective, adequate preparation, time, and a skilled interviewer are required.

7

Plan the Result Outcome

Well begun is half done.

The success of the ABM implementation, like most projects, is determined in the planning stage. Inadequate plans lead to inadequate results. The reasons most often associated with less successful implementations include lost interest/momentum because of long time lines, requirements/expectations not clearly defined and understood, inadequate resources, changing priorities, unexpected crisis, and those implementations simply overcome by events.

Any ABM implementation that commences with a poorly defined expectation/result, inadequate resources, or a time line with initial deliverables a long time away is doomed for failure. Most reasons for failure are avoidable and include those efforts that are overcome by events. A good ABM implementation plan anticipates and eliminates the reasons for failure.

Activity-based management initiatives are successful when they meet the information needs and requirements of the organization. Information becomes valuable when it contributes to meeting the goals, objectives, and strategies of the organization. The failure to link the ABM system to the goals of the organization is fatal. "Build it and they will come" does not apply to ABM implementations because they do not come. The ABM information systems must be built to meet the specific needs of the organization. The purpose and expected results, long term and short term, must be clearly articulated, documented, and understood.

117

The depth and degree of planning required is dependent on the phase of implementation. Early phases of implementation require more planning than later phases. If an overall assessment and implementation plan has been completed, as recommended in Chapter 3, then much of the critical planning has already been done. A competently prepared assessment would have identified overall objectives, goals, and phases of implementation. Planning, in these situations, would be directed toward the specific objectives of the implementation phase being addressed. For those organizations that did not do an overall assessment, considerable work must be completed.

This chapter will cover the critical elements of a good ABM plan. These key elements include the purpose, objectives (deliverables), benefits (results), resources required, project time lines, and the establishment of an implementation team. The key elements are included in two sections of this chapter: balanced planning and teams to achieve end results.

BALANCED PLANNING

There are two important criteria to a balanced ABM implementation plan. First and foremost, the objectives and deliverables of the effort must be aligned with the overall goals and objectives of the organization. As a basic starting point, any major initiative like ABM must contribute to the overall mission and vision of the organization to have value. The second criteria is that ABM project scope, resources, and time lines are balanced in a way that makes meeting the requirements attainable. One person assigned to a one-month effort to define activities for General Motors worldwide is not attainable. Failure to meet the first criteria runs the risk that the efforts expended will be of no value to the organization. Failure to meet the second criteria will create frustration and a loss of project credibility.

In creating a balanced ABM implementation plan, linking and aligning the plan to the organization's goals, missions, vision, and objectives is not particularly difficult. All that is required is a good understanding of the needs, requirements, and direction of the organization. The linkage itself should be quite easy once these are known. For example, if a service company was operating at capacity and turning away business, the need of the organization might be to examine activity capacity as a way to identify bottlenecks and to balance activity capacity. The organization may also need to know the cost of services provided as a way to make better decisions on service mix.

In this example, ABM implementation efforts directed toward identifying non-value-added activities and related cost drivers might not be of immediate value, especially if the elimination of non-value-added activities did not contribute to increasing capacity or lead to better decisions on service mix. What is important is to know the organization's needs and requirements, both long and short term, so that the efforts expended to implement the ABM system are valuable and useful.

The harder part of creating a balanced ABM implementation plan is in balancing the project scope, resources, and time lines with the project deliverables and expectations. The reason this is difficult is simple. Most organizations have not put in an ABM system before, so they have no way to judge whether the plan scope, resources, and time lines are reasonable and attainable. Without experience, balancing project scope with required resources and reasonable time lines is difficult. The result of ABM planning efforts, too often, is the assignment of insufficient resources, extended time lines, or the failure to meet the project deliverables.

That is why we recommend conducting an overall assessment early in the ABM project life cycle to determine, on a preliminary basis, the overall requirements, resources, and time lines necessary to fully implement the ABM system. Based on the assessment, an overall or master plan can be developed and deployed using our four-step model and building block approach. Large organizations choosing to undertake ABM in a significant and aggressive manner might have ten or more implementation teams assigned to various parts of the organization, each doing planning, activity analysis, activity/product costing, data gathering and analysis, and documenting the results for their individual building block. In this implementation environment, planning at both the overall project level and at the building block level are necessary and critical. In a small company or in a limited ABM application where the entire effort might represent just one building block, overall assessments and master plans for implementation are not necessary. The planning for the building block and the entire implementation should be the same.

Estimating the resources required to implement ABM is difficult because of all the variables involved. There are no standard formulas or rules of thumb. In any given situation, the total resources required to implement ABM would have to be based on an assessment of the actual situation as compared to the expectations of the ABM system. Actual situations are company specific and so are expectations. No one starts from the same place, and no one wants the same thing.

Not every company needs ABC to determine the cost of products or services. Many traditional product cost systems provide reliable and accurate cost data. Organizations that have previously undertaken efforts to flowchart and document all significant work process including cause-and-effect analysis to identify the cause of problems, inefficiencies, and costs should not have to do this work over again. These efforts might have also included the identification of performance measures for those work processes deemed to be important. Perhaps all that is needed from ABM in this situation would be its techniques and methods for calculating the actual costs of the activities on a total and per unit of output basis or to identify non-value-added activities and costs. Organizations that have done nothing at all require more work.

Large organizations intending to implement ABM aggressively need to gain experience from the early stages and phases of implementation, so that the overall implementation or master plan can be modified and adjusted to reflect the knowledge gained. This is one of the reasons it is especially important to document the results of efforts for the initial implementation building blocks. In later implementation phases, documenting the results of building block efforts becomes the vital link between analysis and action.

As a starting point and to gain experience, especially in the early stages of the ABM implementation, we recommend a technique to balance resources, time lines, and deliverables where the due date and resources are the independent variables and the scope/deliverables are the dependent variables. By using this technique, the amount of ABM implementation work that can be accomplished in a given time frame with a given resource, and in a given situation, is isolated and identified. This is valuable information and experience that can be used to guide and direct the overall implementation effort.

In applying this technique, start with the time line. The due date should not exceed four months from kickoff. Three months is preferable. Next, realistically determine the available resources for the project effort. It is important to be honest and to avoid wishful thinking here. Available resources include those internal people assigned to the project effort plus whatever external resources are necessary or required. These outside resources could include consultants, software, or both. Given a time line and assigned resources, a simple calculation can be made of the number of equivalent people days available to the project. For example, four internal people assigned 50% of their time to the ABM implementation over a three-month project time line would equate to 132 full-time equivalent days, assuming approximately 66 business days in the three-month period. These full-time equivalent days, plus any outside consulting support, represent the total resource available for the ABM implementation effort.

Now comes the tricky part, selecting a project scope that fits within the constraints of available resources and a predetermined due date or time line. There is a natural tendency to develop an unaggressive project scope. Inexperienced implementors do not want to stick their necks out and will argue that there is a lot of work to be done. Activities have to be specified, output and output measures determined, performance measures established, cost drivers determined, value analysis performed, and costs traced to activities and cost objects. The work itself can sound massive.

For example, the project leader of an ABM implementation located in the midwest was describing all of the work that needed to be done to complete the ABM initiative in one area of the business. The project leader suggested that it would take three months for one full-time person to complete the work. An experienced ABM consultant suggested that while all that was described was true, the effort should not take over three days. After all, the area of the business covered by the project scope consisted of the activities of a single department that included only nine people.

By first establishing a due date and then determining available implementation resources, ABM implementors develop/select a scope of work that can be accomplished during the indicated time period. It is a reiterative process that must be continued until the three pieces are in balance. Because organization and managers often lose interest in projects and initiatives when they do not see tangible results after three to four months of efforts, the due date should be the independent variable. Everything else can change, the due date is a given.

Adjusting the scope of the ABM implementation can be accomplished in many ways. Perhaps the easiest way is to change the number of people and the costs covered in the analysis. Reducing the amount of detail or the level of accuracy required is another way to adjust the project scope to meet the available resources. Eliminating some of the steps in the activity analysis, like developing performance measures and identifying cost drivers, is a third way to adjust the scope of the ABM implementation.

Other required resources that should be part of the plan include the investment of people other than the implementation team members. Time spent on the implementation effort by those people that are being interviewed or by those experts that contribute their time serving to a panel of experts are examples of additional resources required. In addition, any infrastructures required such as steering committees, advisory groups, organizational training, information services personnel for software/computer modeling, and if necessary, outside consulting/advisory services should also be included.

Computer software and consulting services are resources available to support an ABM implementation. These resources enable an organization to reduce the cost and risk of an ABM implementation effort. Use of commercial software significantly reduces the number crunching required and reduces system reporting problems. The experience, knowledge, and expertise an advisory can bring to the table can help avoid dead-ends, pitfalls, and aimless trails that limit the success of the ABM implementation.

When the ABM implementation uses the recommended building block approach and four-step model, each three- to four-month period represents a block of resource available to complete selected parts of the ABM implementation. A scope of effort can be developed that fits the available resources and time lines for each building block. Efforts can be directed to departments, functions, projects, product or product lines, plants, offices, geographical areas, or business processes. The selection is a function of the need, purpose, and objectives for implementing ABM in the organization.

For example, if accurate product cost was the purpose of implementing ABM, then the scope of effort must be addressed toward specific manufacturing plants or areas of manufacturing cost. An ABM implementation objective to determine internal transfer prices would address the support areas of the business. Knowing the resources available and given a due date of three or four months will determine how many plants or how many support departments could be included in the initial project scope.

Each of the examples of specific ABM uses presented in Chapter 2 had a different project scope and objectives. In each case, judgments were made, and areas of the business were selected to begin the implementation. Activity-based management implementation efforts have been directed toward all portions and types of organizations: research and development departments, hospitals, manufacturing plants, distribution facilities, general and administrative people, manufacturing overhead activities, and information systems. As the organization moves along in its ABM implementation, project scope for succeeding phases of work is often determined and recommended at the conclusion of the preceding phase.

Developing a project plan that balances the scope, time lines, and resources available to deliver the expected results and meet the objectives is crucial. It must reflect management's desires and receive their acceptance and agreement. The second critical piece to planning is to establish a team capable of successfully completing the implementation.

TEAMS THAT ACHIEVE THE END RESULT

The ABM implementation team is critical to project success. Successful teams are composed of high-performing people who work well together and have complementary skill sets and an excellent knowledge of the business. Activity-based management has its best chance for success when a cross-functional team is associated with it. The team should be comprised of various disciplines within an organization and include representatives from all departments that have a vested interest in the project outcome (e.g., accounting, production, engineering, marketing).

The members of the cross-functional team will have visibility. The personal credibility of team members lends legitimacy to the activities in which they are involved. Thus, for ABM to be perceived as an organizational priority and an important enterprise, members of the cross-functional team must be well respected by employees and managers. Members of the team must have previously demonstrated an ability to be flexible, innovative, and forward thinking.

The organization's best performers should be encouraged to join the team implementation. The leadership qualities that they bring to the team lend additional credibility. Because these employees often have strong communication skills, they can be the best advocates for the organization's new system. In its early "bumpy" stages, ABM may have to traffic off the goodwill and respect of the team members. In assigning people resources to the teams, the following identifies what to look for and what to avoid:

Look for	Avoid
Results orientation	Negative people
Creativity and innovation	Unreliable people
Willingness to change	Stick-in-the-muds

A team is often no better than its leader. For the ABM implementation leader, more than leadership traits of aggressiveness, integrity, vision, and organization are required. An ABM implementation team leader must be skilled in project management and must have the ability to interface with all levels of the organization.

The team leader must be selected carefully, as the difference between success and failure can often be traced directly to the person who leads the effort and who is responsible for the team effort. Unfortunately, strong team leaders are not generally sitting around waiting for an assignment. The kind of team leader required for the ABM implementation is the same kind of person that everyone wants assigned to projects that are important to the organization. Therefore, as a practical matter, the importance of the ABM effort must be prioritized against the other projects that are important to the organization. In the end, if the effort is not sufficiently important to assign a responsible leader, it would be better to delay the effort than to move forward with inadequate leadership.

Well begun is half done. No truer words have ever been spoken. The ABM implementation plan is the beginning of a successful implementation. It must be done well. Project scope, resources, and time lines must be balanced so the project deliverables and goals are attainable with the resources assigned and the time lines given. The project scope must be linked to the goals, vision, mission, and objectives of the organization if the effort is to create value. These are basic requirements to a successful ABM implementation. In addition, a competent cross-functional team(s) and a capable leader(s) are necessary to execute the implementation plan. An implementation plan, no matter how well prepared, has little chance of success when the people assigned to the effort lack the skills, desire, and abilities necessary to carry it out.

8

Documenting Results

Presentation is everything.

Only when people take action and make decisions based on the knowledge and information gained from the ABM installation can the efforts be declared successful. Absent of action or the decision to make changes, efforts expended in planning, analysis, data gathering, and costing would have produced no value to the organization. Documentation of key findings, recommendations, conclusions, and next steps is a vital link between analysis and action. Properly done, documenting results forms a bridge between the ABM analysis and the costing work, with the actions necessary to effect improvements. In achieving a successful ABM implementation, documenting the result of effort is as important as the balanced implementation plan.

While documentation of ABM implementation results are important, this work should not consume a significant portion of the total implementation resources. The purpose of an ABM implementation is to install a management information system that mirrors the horizontal view of the organization by providing activity-based information and data on significant activities, business processes, and cost objects. Most implementation resources should be directed toward this purpose, as the intent is not to write and produce reports of work done. The report document itself should be regarded as a tool to support the ABM initiative; however, it is not an end in itself.

125

The frequency of documenting and reporting progress and results is a function of the size of the implementation, the culture of the organization, the learning style of its managers, the importance of the effort to the organization, and the comfort level the organization has in the project team responsible for implementation. Some organizations put more emphasis on reports than others and require frequent progress reports, while others will require only documentation at the end of the project. Similarly, some managers want everything in writing, while others only require verbal updates.

Where the activity-based information is critical to short-term decision making or action, it is doubtful management would be willing to wait until the implementation is complete to review preliminary results, conclusions, and recommendations. In these situations, management may want to see progress reports on a regular basis, as the work progresses. The organizations that use our recommended building block approach and four-step ABM implementation model (see Exhibit 3–2) typically issue one report to cover each building block completed.

This chapter will focus on those elements often documented and included in reports. These elements fall under categories of background/understanding and actions/results. But first this chapter will discuss the purpose and value of documenting the results in the report. By understanding the purpose one can better understand the value gained by its preparation. After covering purpose, documentation elements will be addressed.

PURPOSE

In general, there are three purposes of a report document. This first is to communicate the knowledge and information gained. The second is to document what was learned so that others can gain from experience. The third, and most important, is to document recommendations and actions that would improve the organization. These purposes will be discussed further in the following.

Most of the detail knowledge and information gained about activities/processes and products/services is contained in the activity dictionary and in the product/service cost models developed as part of the ABM implementation. This is detailed information often contained in an appendix to the report, with key pieces of knowledge and information contained in the body of the report itself. Key pieces of knowledge and information typically include unprofitable products/services, high cost processes and activities, a ratio of support activities to core activities, a percentage of total resources consumed by non-value-added activities, and significant cost drivers and the cost impact on the organization.

It is also important to document and share experience gained, especially in the early stages of a large ABM initiative. The learning curve for additional phases of ABM implementation can be altered significantly by sharing what works and what does not within the organization. Through implementation, people will identify which data collection techniques work best and where added effort is required to overcome obstacles specific to the company.

The final and most important purpose of the report is to document recommendations, conclusions, and actions that create value to the organization. Documented recommendations and actions are the heart of the report and centerpiece of focus. A well-written and documented report should drive people to action. Early in implementation, presentation is everything. The basis for conclusions and recommendations must be solid, factual, supportable, and believable. Only then will people be motivated to take the recommended actions.

In documenting the result of ABM implementation efforts, two general guidelines are recommended. First, keep the body of the report at 12 pages or less, less being preferable. Be concise and focus on the main points and themes. Exhibits, appendixes, and attachments should be used where appropriate, but the body of the report should not take longer than a magazine article to read. Second, keep the report in draft form until all interested parties have reviewed the documents and provided input. The final document should reflect the resolution of conflict or disagreement and consensus that the information is valid, recommendations are sound, and actions/next steps are correct.

REPORT ELEMENTS

In reviewing the table of contents of many ABM implementation reports, the most common topics include an executive overview or summary; a background on the ABM implementation; a restatement of the project scope, objectives, and deliverables; key findings; method of ABM deployment; major assumptions; recommendations; conclusions; and next steps. These topics are the key elements that are often documented in any phase of the ABM implementation.

Key elements of a report can be broadly divided into two parts. The first part includes those elements that relate to background and understanding: assumptions, method of deployment, resources used, scope, objectives, and deliverables. The second part includes those elements that relate to results achieved: recommendations, conclusions, key findings, and next steps. In any given report, part will be used to convey background and understanding, and part will convey the result of effort. Some people like to address results first, followed by background and supporting information. Others prefer to lay out background and understanding before discussing the results of the implementation. What comes first is a matter of preference. Both parts are required for full understanding and comprehension.

Before getting into the many key elements of the implementation report, many organizations find it useful to include an executive summary or overview. This summary accommodates the readers that will not take the time to read an entire report or those that are only interested in an overview. The executive summary should cover the two or three most significant items in detail, avoiding the use of a broad brush to provide a superficial review of all the findings and recommendations. After the summary, the background and understanding and results achieved parts of the report, discussed below, are addressed.

Background and Understanding

Providing background on ABM methods, philosophies, and practices is an important area to cover in the report and is dependent on the knowledge level of the intended reviewer. To perform an adequate review of the result of an ABM effort requires some level of base knowledge and understanding. While the purpose is not to fully educate the reviewer on the principals, methods, and philosophies of ABC and ABM, a paragraph or two should be sufficient to provide a minimum level of context and understanding.

An example, taken from a final report, used definitions to provide a base level of knowledge, as follows: "Activity-based costing (ABC) is a methodology to determine the true cost of activities, processes, and the products/services of a business. ABC is a product/service costing tool. Activity-based management (ABM) is focused not only on the cost of activities and products/services but also how to improve performance. ABM uses value-added and non-value-added analysis, cost driver identification, and performance measures to drive process improvement opportunities and improve decision making. Simply stated, ABM is the collection and reporting of cost and operation information about the activities of the business—what people and machines actually do every day. ABM provides an organized way for a business or business function to look at their effectiveness and efficiency, to determine the cause of cost, and to establish relevant measures of activity performance in terms of cost, quality, and time."

Provided the scope, objectives, and deliverables of the implementation effort were adequately documented and communicated during the planning phase, a concise restatement of these areas is all that is required. This restatement should be no more than one or two pages in length. Where these areas were not adequately documented and communicated or in situations where people are confused as to the intent of these areas, a more detailed discussion may be required.

A brief overview of the method of ABM deployment, especially as it relates to method(s) of data gathering, is important. How did the team gather information? Who did they talk to? Who was on the implementation team? What level of consensus was achieved? By documenting the methods and sources of data used in the analysis, two good things happen:

1. Provided the methods and sources of data are reliable, appropriate, and relevant, credibility is established, and managers have confidence in the end result.

2. Acknowledging the role people played in contributing to the effort is a nice way to say thank-you.

Assumptions that are critical to a full, comprehensive understanding of the key findings, conclusions, and recommendations must be documented. As a minimum, the major activity and resource drivers used to trace costs should be disclosed. The percentage of costs that were traced, as opposed to allocated, should be stated. The basis of estimates, when used and significant, should be documented. Any significant assumptions made as to the validity of data entering the system should be discussed. Finally, when in doubt about whether to include an assumption, put it in. It does not have to take up a large part of the report, just a sentence or two.

Results Achieved

Key findings, recommendations, conclusions, and next steps are the heart of the ABM report. These elements of the project report document the results achieved. Key findings and conclusions cover the significant learning that resulted from the ABM analysis and costing efforts. Key findings should cover the high points of the analysis. Typical key findings include the following:

1. The number of activities identified as part of the project scope.

2. Total costs (monthly, quarterly, or yearly) of resources consumed to execute the activities, together with identification of major cost components (people, equipment, facilities, etc.) used in the activity.

3. Specific identification of activities with the highest cost—those that account for 35 to 50% of the total costs consumed, together with the cost per unit of activity output.

4. Percentage relationships of activities deemed core or primary as compared with secondary or support. For example, the relationship might be 60/40, where 60% of the total dollars is spent on core activities, and the remainder is spent on supporting activities.

5. The dollar amount of non-value-added activities and the relationship of value added to nonvalue added. For example, the ratio might be 65/35, where 65% of the dollars is spent on value-added activities, and the remainder is spent on non-value-added activities. To the extent that non-value-added tasks of value-added activities were identified and quantified, this information should also be included as a key finding.

6. Significant cost drivers should be identified and reviewed in the report.

7. New measures of activity performance should be documented.

8. Activities that were identified as targets for improvements should be discussed.

9. Key findings with respect to product/product line profitability should be expressed. Examples of differences between traditional and activity-based product/service cost should be documented and presented in the report as a key finding.

Recommendations and next steps generally fall into three areas. The first is to take action on the knowledge and information gained. Someone has to do something. The second area is recommendations and next steps for ongoing systems implementation. Finally, the report should contain recommendations to integrate ABM information with existing methods and systems.

It would be highly unusual for a skillfully conducted ABM analysis to have not identified significant potential for improvement. The payback for efforts expended is achieved when people take action or decisions that result in organizational improvement. If the project planning was adequately done, a method of handing off responsibility to effect the identified improvements would already be completed. Next steps belong to the people responsible for the improvement initiative.

In those situations where the report represents initial ABM efforts, recommendations for the ongoing systems implementation can be quite extensive. Procedures and methods for collecting data will be required. Decisions as to the frequency of reporting, levels of reporting, and responsibility for system maintenance must be made. In more advanced ABM implementations, recommendations might be limited to those that relate to collecting new information.

To realize the full benefit of ABM it must be integrated with the mainstream of the organization. Full integration, which takes years to achieve, means that ABM information is used for operating decisions, strategy development, capital expenditure analysis, improvement initiatives, and measuring performance and is reflected in individual and team compensation. Report recommendations, with respect to integration, typically take the form of linking ABM with selected parts of the firm's infrastructure. For example, the report might contain a recommendation to link activity performance with a gain sharing program (i.e., sharing of gains associated with activity improvements) that might be in place.

Integration recommendations should cover the use of activity-based performance measures and the relationship to the overall performance measures used by the organization. Unless the system is already in place, it will be necessary to establish a method and procedures for reporting activity performance. In addition, goals and benchmarks of activity performance must be developed.

While this is a good summary of the topic elements most often included in the final report, it should not be considered all inclusive. Every ABM implementation is different, and the emphasis, topics, and elements to be covered are application and organization specific. Further, the stage of implementation will dictate both the content and the level of detail contained in the report. Implementations that are far along in their life cycle may find it necessary to cover only key findings, conclusions, recommendations, and next steps. Writer discretion is advised.

9

Examples of Specific Real-Life Implementation Situations

The implementation methods, techniques, and approaches outlined in this book are generic in the sense that no two implementations are exactly the same. Implementors of ABM information systems must adapt the general philosophies, principles, methods, and steps to the specific requirement of the organization. There is no cookbook to implementing ABM. Rather, the tools, methods, and techniques are used in different ways for different organizations, depending on the situation and specific requirements.

This chapter will address ten applications of ABM where the intent was often beyond ABC. These applications were selected to provide the reader with a wide range of example. From an effort driven by the commander of a 65,000 person defense organization to a grassroots effort started by a member of a finance department. From a limited assessment to a company-wide implementation. From a product cost emphasis to a process cost emphasis. From a company recognized by CAM-I, APQC, and the IBC for its best practices in ABM to a company whose initiative was overcome by events.

The examples include the DLA, Acxiom Corporation, Phillips Petroleum, National Demographics and Lifestyles Inc. (NDL), Mallinckrodt Medical, National Semiconductor, SEMATECH, Union Pacific Resources

Corporation, Shaffer, and Caterair International. This chapter will focus on the actual method of deployment used by each company together with the key learnings.

DEFENSE LOGISTICS AGENCY

The DLA of the U.S. DOD is responsible for the supply, management, and distribution of over 4 million line items of supply required by all four branches of the U.S. armed forces. Through their participation in the CAM-I CMS task force, the DOD has been interested in the principles of ABM, as they applied to the department and to its principle suppliers. The DLA, like all agencies associated with the DOD, was under pressure to reduce the scope of its operations to correspond with the reduction of U.S. military presence. Under the leadership of the DLA Director, VADM Edward M. Straw and his Principal Deputy, MGen Lawrence P. Farrell, the DLA undertook a pilot project at its Defense Industrial Supply Center in Philadelphia, Pennsylvania. The Defense Industrial Supply Center completed its implementation over a three-month period, which commenced on April 1, 1993 and was completed on July 1, 1993. The results of this initial pilot effort were successful, and in August of 1993 the agency was directed to undertake ABM worldwide. All DLA sites were instructed to complete their activity-based analysis and to issue their initial reports, complete with recommendations for improvement, by April 1, 1994. At the time, this implementation was the largest, most significant implementation ever conducted in the United States. Each DLA business area commander was responsible to define the activities under their command and deliver the following:

1. Cost of activities.
2. Classification of each activity as value added, mandatory nonvalue added, or nonmandatory nonvalue added.
3. Cost of the business processes (cost objects).
4. Identification of cost drivers.
5. Performance measures for each activity.
6. Recommendations for improvement and actions to be taken.

Purpose of Effort

The purposes of the effort were as follows:

1. The DLA was committed to continuous process improvement and needed a measurement tool so that DLA management could judge how well their improvement efforts were working.
2. The DLA command wanted a tool to put in place that would give local operating managers the visibility to take the cuts and reductions necessary in areas that were not critical to mission objectives.
3. The agency wanted to augment its current unit cost reduction/optimization efforts.

The primary benefit expected from the ABM was in better decisions on activities that could be eliminated or reduced during a period of downsizing and reduction.

The activity-based project at the DLA included all activities and processes associated with the supply operations, defense contract management command, and depot warehouses. In addition, the defense reutilization and defense fuels were also included in the project scope. The effort included the activities of the 65,000 employees of the command. The total resources required to conduct this implementation involved approximately ten people years of effort (2,400 days) from internal personnel working on implementation teams and 150 days of external consulting resources used primarily for training.

Implementation and Deployment

The sheer size of this initiative required a very structured approach to implementation and a considerable amount of planning. First, a program manager responsible for the overall ABM implementation was selected from the DLA headquarters and assigned a small staff of support people. The program manager was responsible for the overall planning, coordination, training, and administration required by this effort. The program manager was assigned early in the process and given wide latitude to investigate the potential uses, benefits, applications, and requirements of ABM within the DLA and to pilot and test ABM within the agency. The overall implementation included 20 milestone events over an 18-month period commencing in January 1993. The first milestone event was ABM training to DLA senior level management. The final milestone event was a briefing by each business area commander as to the results of the implementation.

All implementation efforts were the responsibility of project leaders and project team members employed by the agency. For each of the business units (defense supply centers, defense contract management command, defense distribution and support areas), project leaders were identified and participated in an intensive five-day training session designed specifically for their business unit. Each team leader was trained in the principles, methods, philosophies, and steps required to implement ABM. As part of the five-day workshop, team leaders developed a preliminary ABM implementation plan for their area of responsibility.

At the conclusion of the training, each team leader returned to their respective site and finalized the implementation plan and selected team members for additional training. At each individual site, project teams were given two days of training in the principles, methods, philosophies, uses, and steps to complete the ABM initiative.

The specific steps involved in the implementation at each site included the following:

1. Define activities. The DLA utilized as much of its existing data as possible in defining activities. For example, within the defense supply centers, a substantive effort had taken place previously to develop models and flowcharts of each of the areas of the business.

2. Define outputs for the activities. In the agency these were known as work counts.

3. Trace costs to the activities. Detailed cost codes were traced individually to activities.

4. Determine cost drivers. Both internal and external cost drivers were identified. External cost drivers were segregated as DLA related, congressional, or environmental.

5. Determine performance measures. Key and significant activities were linked to defined business area performance measures.

6. Perform value analysis and identify areas for improvement.

The Current Situation

Results of the DLA implementation efforts were completed by April 1, 1994 and presented to the DLA commander shortly thereafter. Each individual unit prioritized the improvement opportunities and assigned teams to implement the changes and improvements required. The agency continues to report activity-based information on a monthly basis and uses the information to support its benchmarking and reengineering initiatives.

ACXIOM CORPORATION

Acxiom Corporation, located in Conway, Arkansas, is a publicly held company just 20 miles outside of Little Rock, Arkansas. A rapid growing company, Acxiom has annual sales of approximately $200 million and employs 2,000 people. Acxiom is a service company that manages marketing databases for other companies. In addition they also provide outsourcing services for data processing departments. Their client list includes TransUnion, The American Management Association, Citibank, and Bank of America.

In 1991 Acxiom Corporation initiated a very extensive quality improvement initiative which they called Race for Excellence (RFE). In order to create a sense of innovation, creativity, and entrepreneurial spirit, Acxiom Corporation was initially interested in ABM as a way to establish transfer prices for services performed by support departments to the operating or business units. For example, in the accounting area, the president wanted accounting personnel to think of their services from the customers standpoint and to operate their department in much the same manner that a local CPA firm would operate in serving its client base. In addition, they were interested in utilizing ABM to augment and support their RFE initiatives. Subsequently, after personnel had been trained in the principles and philosophies of ABM, the focal point of their efforts was directed to support improvement initiatives. Activity-based management was intended to support RFE in the following ways:

♦ Continuous Process Improvement

To provide an organized way to look at the effectiveness and efficiency of all processes and to select those areas for improvement that will result in the greatest initial benefit.

To determine the cost drivers of each process/activity so that improvement efforts can be directed and focused toward prevention.

To provide basic and fundamental cost and performance information about processes and activities used to judge the result of RFE improvement efforts.

◆ Activity and Service Costing

To provide cost information about processes and activities.

To provide cost information for products and services that can be used for pricing and investment decisions.

To establish the cost of service activities provided by support functions to operating business units.

◆ Performance Measurement

To provide individual and business unit performance measures that reflect what the individual and business units control.

To link individual and business unit performance measures to Acxiom objectives.

By defining and quantifying the actual expenditures for activities and work processes performed, management believed that knowledge would create a passion to control cost. They believed that by quantifying non-value-added work and by identifying the dollar amount of duplication and rework performed, operating personnel would be more inclined to effect the necessary improvements. In addition, they believed activity-based performance measures would begin to drive and support a change in culture and behavior toward managing key and significant activities from a quality, cycle time, and cost standpoint. By focusing on these three items, they felt they would better serve their customers.

The objectives of the effort were to identify all business processes and activities, to determine an internal service cost for transfer pricing, and to identify opportunities for improvement. The scope of effort included all of the operations and personnel located in Conway, Arkansas. Conway, Arkansas accounted for over 80% of the personnel, revenues, and costs of the consolidated operations.

Implementation and Deployment

Activity-based management was initially implemented in two phases at the main operating location, which accounted for most of the total personnel and costs of the consolidated operations. Phase I was directed toward the continuous process improvement and activity/product costing aspects of supporting the organization's RFE initiatives. Approximately one person year (240 days) of internal team resources and 65 days of external consulting days were required over the three-month time line for phase I. Phase II was directed toward performance measurement and improvement of the base ABM reporting system. The organization utilized a seven-person project team (six internal and one external consultant/facilitator), each of whom devoted approximately 50% of their time to the effort over the three-month phase I implementation time line. The project leader devoted 100% of time to the effort. The project team reported to the senior executive staff of Acxiom.

Acxiom is organized in approximately 20 business units, each headed by a business unit leader. Business units could be revenue generating or support. Business unit leaders are responsible for operating business units in an innovative, creative, entrepreneurial, and profitable way. Meeting the information requirement needs of each business unit was imperative, for they were the primary users of ABM information. In essence, an ABM information system was required for each business unit. Accordingly, the following specific deliverables for phase I were required for each business unit.

- Identify the key and significant activities for each Acxiom Corporation business unit.
- For each key and significant activity, determine the following:

  Description/definition

  Output

  Output measure

  Cost

  Cost driver

  Input (trigger)

  Performance measurements

  Activity attributes (value added, nonvalue added, primary, strategic, etc.)
- Business process relationship map linking activities to business processes.
- Ranking of activities for improvement.
- Summary, conclusions, recommendations, and next steps.

The roles and responsibilities for the project team and management and business unit leaders were as follows:

Project Team
- Perform all of the interviews, data gathering, and analysis necessary to form the basis, results, and conclusions contained in the project deliverables.

♦ Facilitate consensus on the key and significant activities.

♦ Prepare project status for management review.

Management and Business Unit Leaders

♦ Identify a person from the company responsible for the success of the project.

♦ Be available on a timely basis for interviews.

♦ Provide rapid responses to requests for information.

♦ Meet with the project team at predetermined dates with minimal interruptions.

♦ Assign resources as required to meet project objectives.

The overall implementation plan at Acxiom for phase I involved the following eight steps:

1. Prepare the detailed ABM implementation plan.
2. Assign project team.
3. Training/work session for key personnel and project team.
4. Interviews and analysis to define activities, outputs, measures, cost drivers, tracing methodology, and activity attributes for each business unit.
5. Activity and service cost tracing.
6. Prepare draft of report, including conclusions, recommendations, and next steps.
7. Review of final draft of report with management.
8. Deliver final report.

Activity analysis and activity costing (steps 4 and 5) were required for each of the company's 20 business units. Accordingly, most of the team resources and efforts were directed toward this part of the implementation plan. The phase I time line commenced with a two-day training/work session for key personnel and project team members and was attended by senior management and business unit leaders.

The content of this two-day management workshop was divided 40% toward an ABM overview and the basic steps to implement and 30% toward ABM implementation in Acxiom. The remaining 30% was directed toward group exercises to identify, on a very preliminary basis, business processes and key activities for Acxiom. Five groups of participants were formed (5 to 6 participants per group) and asked to describe the total business in terms of 8 to 12 business processes and to document the business processes in a relationship map. Examples of business process relationship maps from other organizations were provided to stimulate creativity and to serve as example. While there was a substantial latitude of perspective on the business processes, after discussion the combined group reached preliminary consensus on their business processes. Each group was then assigned one or more business processes and asked to identify (again on a preliminary basis) the 5 to 10 most significant activities associated with that business process. The resulting workshop product, a "straw man" of business processes and key activities, served as a framework and common understanding that would be changed, modified, validated, and verified by analysis, as the implementation proceeded. That portion of training directed toward establishing business processes and key activities is an example of the panel of experts technique to gather data where the managers are the experts and the data to be gathered are a preliminary listing of business processes and activities.

The project team used group-based data collection techniques in the activity analysis and activity costing (steps 4 and 5) for some business units. Key people from each area of the business unit were involved in workshops to define activities, do value-added analysis, identify cost drivers, and provide the information on how people spend their time and how resources are used so that activities could be costed. The total number of people involved in these workshops was about 10% of total employees. Each employee who participated contributed about one day to the effort.

Key findings resulting from the phase I effort included the following:

1. A total of 137 key and significant activities of the Conway-based business units were identified.
2. The top five activities consumed 38% of the payroll-related costs of the Conway-based business units. The top 25 activities consumed 74% of the total payroll and related cost.
3. One business process accounted for 35% of total cost.
4. Two non-value-added activities accounted for over 40 to 45% of costs of some revenue business units.
5. Insufficient activity resources were being deployed to a critical business process.

6. Skill level of associates and inadequate planning/requirements definition were two of the most significant cost drivers.

7. In many cases, software development groups had difficulty describing their customer. They were not able to easily track their products to the final user and therefore did not have a systematic way to get customer feedback. Activities needed to be added.

8. The transition of new products from R&D into full use by the software groups was listed as a key activity of R&D, but not by the software groups. This affected the speed and priority of new product introduction.

Over 20 additional observations and recommendations were made.

The goal of phase II was to implement ABM into Acxiom's mainstream of operational and financial management. Specific deliverables included the following:

1. Train and educate key personnel on ABM principles, process improvement skills, and performance measurement.

2. Refine the activity dictionary and gain consensus on performance measures.

3. Enhanced internal systems for data capture to allow for ABM reporting and product costing.

4. Develop initial ABM reporting formats.

Five training seminars were conducted, which included approximately 40 people in each. The level of people trained included business unit executives, team leaders, and key personnel in each business unit. Each business unit executive was challenged to take the skills gained in the training and to apply those skills in their units by mapping one or two key activities.

During phase II, the company met with each business unit executive and developed a set of customer-driven performance measures. Performance measurement work consisted of first developing an integrated, customer-driven, performance measurement model to link the overall company's strategic vision and goals to performance measures and requirements for customers, associates, managers, executives, and other stakeholders. Performance measures were developed for each business unit. In conjunction with a corporate measurements task force, these measurements were validated and linked with gain-sharing objectives.

An extensive part of the phase II effort involved the enhancement, modification, and adjustments to internal systems to provide the necessary data included in ABM reports. This effort is ongoing but did not require the full ABM implementation team; therefore, the team was disbanded. Responsibility for next steps remained with the project leader, who was responsible for the following:

1. To deliver and respond to the business unit reporting needs.
2. To roll out ABM to an off-site location(s).
3. To provide additional training on ABM, process improvement, and performance measurement.

The Current Situation

Acxiom is a good example of an organization that used a building block approach to ABM implementation. The first two phases of implementation were in essence two of the building blocks required to complete the ABM installation. At the end of phase II the implementation team was disbanded and the project leader was assigned responsibility for the ongoing collection and reporting of ABM information. Phases III and IV (two more building blocks) were subsequently undertaken to substantially improve the ABM reporting capabilities and to drive the integration of ABM with the culture, values, and goals of the organization. In April 1995, Acxiom was selected as a best practice site in a landmark ABM best practice study jointly conducted by the APQC, IBC, and CAM-I.

PHILLIPS PETROLEUM

Phillips Petroleum is a fully integrated oil company based in Bartlesville, Oklahoma. In terms of total sales, Phillips Petroleum ranks number 66 on the "Business Week 1000" with annual sales of approximately $13 to $14 billion. Total assets are approximately $10 to $11 billion. Phillips Petroleum has undertaken activity-based initiatives in several parts of its operations. The purpose of the project effort described here was directed toward the research and engineering function for the company's operations that made plastic resin. The research and engineering support function was responsible for the testing of plastic parts made from their material and for the materials themselves. The research and engineering support function was responsible for four distinct operating areas of the company, each focused on a different kind of plastic.

Expenses of the research and engineering function were allocated to these operating divisions based upon a percentage of sales, which was unacceptable to the operating managers of the business areas. Research and development management personnel were interested in understanding the true cost of their services (the tests that were performed) so that cost estimates could be provided to operating people before work began and as basis to charge for the services performed.

There were two purposes of this effort. The first purpose was to determine the true cost of services performed by the research and engineering department. The second purpose was to build a forecasting model that enabled company personnel to estimate the cost of performing services (tests) so that operating people could make judgments based on true cost information, prior to committing resources. Management expected to benefit from this implementation in two ways:

1. By understanding the activities associated with their services, support personnel could focus on improving the activities performed as a way of reducing the cost of services.

2. By knowing the true cost of services utilized, operating personnel would be in a better position to make judgment as to the cost benefit of their testing requirements.

The three primary deliverables of this project were to determine the actual cost of the activities and services performed by the function, to flowchart the activities performed for each service, and to build a forecasting model based on activities and activity cost. The scope of effort included all research and development activities performed by the plastic resin test and the engineering people located in Bartlesville, Oklahoma. The total number of personnel included in the project scope was 90. The total equivalent implement team days required was approximately 24, conducted over a six-week time line. External consulting and advisory services to support this initiative was approximately 15 days.

Implementation and Deployment

The company utilized an eight-person work team that met regularly over the six-week time span. The effort commenced in mid-November of

1992 and was completed by year-end. A total of five meetings was held by the project team. The meetings each lasted about half of a day and were designed to move the effort along by (1) reviewing the result of the previous meeting assignments and (2) assigning specific actions and tasks for completion by the next scheduled meeting. Modifications or changes to presented material that resulted from discussion were included with meeting minutes, published within 24 hours of the meeting. Meeting minutes were limited to one page, plus any necessary attachments.

Because this project was fairly condensed and involved the work efforts of only 90 to 95 people, deployment was relatively easy and straightforward. A seven-step action plan was developed, responsibilities were assigned, and due dates were established. The steps of action were as follows:

STEP	DESCRIPTION
1.	Interview key personnel in the Plastics Technical Center (PTC) Operations and in the Materials Evaluation Laboratory to determine key and significant work processes, work process outputs, resources consumed by key and significant work processes, and cost drivers.
2.	Perform additional data gathering and analysis to reach consensus on key and significant activities to be costed.
3.	Using year-to-date actual costs and actual work activity outputs, determine the cost per unit of output for each key and significant work process.
4.	Review current work order system and make recommendations for a single work order system to log work requests through the PTC Operations and Material Evaluation Laboratory.
5.	Review workload and sequence of process steps performed by the operations group. Define specific requirements and needs associated with operations scheduling.
6.	Develop a PC-based system to estimate the activity costs associated with requests for work orders.
7.	Evaluate three PC-based scheduling systems and any existing systems used within Phillips, and make recommendations of which system meets the needs and requirements of the PTC.

The Current Situation

In this limited ABM application company personnel continue to update the database of actual cost and output information for their activities. This enables them to monitor performance against standards and expectations. For about 80% of the requests from operating business units for testing, estimates of costs are prepared and furnished to operating managers. The number of requests has been reduced, which is largely attributable to better cost/benefit analysis by operation managers.

NATIONAL DEMOGRAPHICS AND LIFESTYLES, INC.

National Demographics and Lifestyles, Inc. (NDL) is a Denver-based organization that processes warranty card information sent to it by the customer of the product manufacturer. NDL has annual sales of approximately $20 million and employs 300 people. Their basic business involves collecting approximately 35 million warranty cards each year and entering that data into a database. The information collected includes information about the product and demographic and lifestyle information on the person sending in the card. Once processed, information about the product and the consumer is sent to the manufacturer. Lifestyle and demographic information is maintained in databases and enhanced in a way to provide valuable mailing lists to organizations in the direct mail industry. One of the first service companies in the nation to implement ABM, NDL's efforts consisted of two phases. Phase I was to examine the activities for a portion of the business called data entry. A significant amount of cost is incurred in this area of the business and was a good place to experiment and test ABM. For NDL, phase I was a pilot effort. In phase II, the organization defined business processes and activities company wide as a way to select business processes for improvement and renovation.

The purpose of the overall effort (phases I and II combined) was as follows:

1. Develop a business process relationship map that described the inter-relationships of business processes at NDL.
2. Define key and significant activities associated with each business process.
3. Estimate costs associated with individual business processes and activities.

4. For significant activities, determine cost drivers, performance measures, and value added.

5. Prioritize and select activities for improvement and renovation.

The scope of phase I included only those activities associated with the data entry department. The scope of phase II included all processes and activities performed by NDL company wide. The expected benefits from this implementation were to enable managers to assign resources to those business processes where improvement would result in the greatest benefit.

Implementation and Deployment

The implementation and deployment of phase I involved a six-person team consisting of members of the data entry department and members of the finance area. Based on one-on-one interviews, activities were defined for the department. The final result was that six activities were defined and analyzed for this area of the business. The implementation and deployment of phase II involved three key people from the management team at NDL. Based upon their knowledge and understanding of the business, they prepared a first draft of a business process relationship map and a preliminary identification of key and significant activities. This information was presented to management as a way to obtain consensus and agreement. A number of modifications were made before final consensus was reached.

Activity costing was accomplished by asking each department manager to estimate, to the best of their ability, the percent of resources expended in each business process area. Based upon those percentages (resource drivers), the total cost of individual business processes and activities was calculated. Additional analysis was performed, and ultimately three business processes were selected for redesign.

The Current Situation

The members of the data entry department continue to provide information about the activities that they perform and to track those activities against selected performance criteria. Activities are monitored and controlled on a monthly basis.

With respect to phase II, the result was the deployment of resources and efforts toward the improvement of selected business processes. The current situation at NDL is a good example of how Activity-Based Management information can be used to drive improvement efforts.

MALLINCKRODT CARDIOLOGY

Mallinckrodt is a St. Louis–based manufacturer and supplier of medical products to the health care industry. The cardiology division sells, manufacturers, and distributes catheters to medical professionals. The product is manufactured in Angleton, Texas. The ABM implementation was undertaken in this manufacturing facility to support its TQM initiatives and to gain a better understanding of the plant's overhead. For the plant's continuous improvement efforts to be successful, a system to provide timely, accurate, and relevant information as to the performance of the key and significant activities was required. The ABM implementation supported Angleton's improvement efforts by providing the following:

♦ An organized way to look at the effectiveness and efficiency of all the business processes and underlying activities at the plant and to highlight those areas for improvement that will yield the greatest benefit.

♦ Identification of the cost drivers for key and significant activities so that improvement efforts can be directed toward cost reduction through redesign of the business processes and key activities.

♦ Basic and fundamental cost and performance information about processes and activities to judge how well the improvement efforts are working.

♦ Basic understanding of where the time and dollars of the overhead departments were being spent.

The expected results and benefits were as follows:

♦ To identify specific areas to be targeted for review by a continuous improvement team.

♦ To improve management reporting and to provide better information for decision making.

♦ To develop performance measures that would perpetuate continuous improvement attitudes.

The overall mission was to support the TQM process by developing and implementing an ABM reporting system at the Angleton facility. The goal was to develop a reporting system that will enable the TQM effort to identify the value-added and non-value-added activities and to direct efforts toward reducing or eliminating the non-value-added activities. Accomplishments of this mission would result in lower standard costs and, therefore, higher gross margins, better utilization of plant resources, and an increase in overall customer satisfaction that translated into increased market share.

The scope of effort included all key processes and activities performed by 200 people at the Angleton facility. These processes and activities were to account for 90% of total cost.

Implementation and Deployment

This implementation effort was performed during the period July 1992 to February 1993. The ABM project team included two people: the plant controller and a financial staff person from the corporate office. Each person devoted two to three days a month to the project effort. Assistance from an outside consultant was also utilized. The overall project scope covered all business processes and the underlying key and significant activities performed at the Angleton facility and covered costing those processes and activities based on the fiscal year 1992 actual results. Specific deliverables included the following:

- ◆ Identification of the main business processes and the key and significant activities at the Angleton facility.
- ◆ For each key and significant activity, determine the following:
  Description and definition
  Tasks
  Customers (internal/external) of the activity
  Cost drivers
  Output measures
  Performance measures
  Departments involved
- ◆ Business process relationship map.
- ◆ Comparison of traditional costing to ABC.

- ◆ Ranking of activities for improvement.
- ◆ Summary, conclusions, and recommendations.

Interviews were conducted with the managers and the key employees of each department. The purposes of the interviews were to identify and define the main business processes and the underlying key and significant activities at the plant, to identify the outputs and customers of the activity, and to determine potential cost drivers and performance measures of each activity.

Payroll-related expenses were allocated to the activities based upon a percentage breakdown of employee time based upon each department's input. Non-payroll-related items were traced to the activities based upon appropriate methodologies.

Key Findings

Key findings resulting from the ABM effort included the following:

1. A total of 48 key and significant activities were identified. These activities were summarized into nine business processes.

2. On a cost basis, the top five activities consumed 38% of the total costs (excluding raw materials). The top 12 activities consumed 59% of total cost.

3. One business process accounted for 32% of the total cost.

4. The manufacturing operations support business process was 69% of the product manufacturing business process. For every dollar of manufacturing cost, 69 cents was required in support.

5. Non-value-added activities totaled 28% of total cost.

6. A summary of the primary business processes/activities, as compared with secondary (support) business processes and activities, was 56% primary and 44% secondary.

7. Significant cost drivers that affected many business processes/activities included the following:

   Complexity of product design

   Regulatory requirements

   Complexity of process

   Documentation requirements

   Product and/or process specifications/tolerance

8. The company spent a significant amount of money on the activity of developing process improvements. The level of spending could not be recaptured in improvements to product manufacturing. In addition, because the output of the activity was engineering change orders, this activity was increasing process complexity, which was identified as a major cost driver to the organization.

9. No one individual or group was fully responsible for the key business processes at Angleton. To effect continuous improvement of processes and products, it was necessary to assign a person or project team to product lines and key processes to ensure that attention was given to improving the product/process, eliminating non-value-added activities, and reducing costs.

The Current Situation

This application of ABM is a good example of its use as a strategic tool. Activity information is collected and updated as frequently as necessary to monitor, direct, and support Angleton's improvement initiatives. It is also a good example of using ABM tools and techniques to assess and analyze an organization's performance.

NATIONAL SEMICONDUCTOR

National Semiconductor is a Fortune 500 company that designs, markets, sells, manufactures, and distributes semiconductors. It is one of the top ten semiconductor manufacturers in the world. They are a global manufacturer with two major operating entities: Communications and Computing and Standard Product Group. Wafer fabs are located in the United States, Scotland, and Israel. Assembly/test facilities are in the United States, Singapore, Malaysia, Philippines, and Japan.

One of the Fabs in the Logic Division of the Standard Products Group is located in Portland, Maine. During 1993, the Portland Fab embraced an ABC product costing implementation effort. Although directed toward product costing, this effort was part of a larger initiative at National Semiconductor that centered around the collection and reporting of ABM information used to improve the effectiveness and efficiency of the organization. This initiative was focused and directed toward using ABC methods, techniques, and procedures to determine accurate product/process costs of MIL/AERO Logic Level S products. MIL/AERO Level

S products are space level semiconductors used in the most demanding of situations where chip performance is critical. The project sponsor was the MIL/AERO Logic Level S Product line director. The effort commenced on June 28, 1993 and was completed on August 17, 1993.

The primary purpose of the MIL/AERO product costing project was to calculate a more accurate manufacturing cost for S Level logic products. That information was required to do the following:

♦ Establish minimum sales prices.

♦ Allocate production and other resources to the most profitable products.

♦ Determine manufacturing priorities.

♦ Establish service pricing.

♦ Make decisions on products that may be eliminated, pruned, or de-emphasized.

By directing plant manufacturing resources toward the most profitable market opportunities, net profit would be increased. Accurate product cost information was vital to reaching product mix decisions and setting priorities. The scope of work included all MIL/AERO Logic Level S processes/products manufactured in South Portland. The primary deliverable was a Bill of Activities—a costed list of the key and significant activities associated with the South Portland operation. The secondary deliverable was a representative sample of costed Logic Level S products derived by using the costed Bill of Activities.

Implementation and Deployment

This effort was conducted over a six-week period using a nine-person implementation team where each team member contributed six to eight days to the effort. The project leader played an active role and contributed 12 to 15 days. Outside consulting resources were utilized to assist and guide the management and the team. The overall approach was to complete each of the major work steps in the following sequential order:

Step 1. Establish and document an achievable implementation plan.

Step 2. Training of project team.

Step 3. Activity analysis.

Step 4. Activity costing.

Step 5. Product costing.

Step 6. Issue results and recommendations for next steps.

Project planning (step 1)

The preliminary plan was developed by the management consulting firm and approved by the company. The implementation plan was based on standard ABC methods, enhanced for special considerations at MIL/AERO, such as the impact recent downsizing had on historical data. This plan was reviewed, modified, and approved by the project team.

Training (step 2)

Training occurred on the first two days of the project. Key personnel in the MIL/AERO organization attended the first day of training while the project team members attended both days. The training agenda included the following:

1st Day	2nd Day
ABM/ABC overview (principles/concepts)	Implementation plan review/modification
Preliminary identification of key and significant activities (group brainstorming exercises)	Costing methodologies to be used

Activity analysis (step 3)

The purpose of the activity analysis was to determine and define key and significant activities associated with the manufacture of Logic Level S products. Fifty percent of the total personnel (88) that comprise the MIL/AERO South Portland operation were interviewed. Interviews were conducted at a detail level sufficient to provide the information necessary to segregate the people resource between Logic and non-Logic operations. Activities were defined and documented for assembly/environmental/finish, test & burn-in, customer programs, and planning and engineering support departments. Activities associated with corporate allocated costs were excluded from the activity analysis.

In total, 85 MIL/AERO key and significant activities were identified and defined. For each key and significant activity, the following information was obtained and documented:

1. Definition/description of activity.
2. Level—unit, batch/lot, product, event, etc.—at which an activity occurs.
3. Output—result of activity.
4. Output measure—quantity of outputs.
5. Time to perform each activity.
6. Output volumes—number of outputs in a given time period.

Activity and product costing (steps 4 and 5)

For the ABM implementor, activity and product costing at MIL/AERO was a technical challenge. Several key assumptions and analysis were required. Key assumptions, together with the rationale and method of use were as follows:

1. Financial forecasts were used for resource costing purposes. Other time frame data was not appropriate since all but the forecast included some "predownsizing" MIL/AERO activities and costs.
2. MIL/AERO costs were captured in total for logic, discreet, and linear products. This effort was directed to Logic Level products only. Estimated production requirements had to be analyzed to determine the relationship of Logic Level S use of manufacturing resources compared with the total use. Only those resources that pertained to logic products were to be traced to logic activities.
3. Estimated activity outputs. For unit and batch/lot activities, the production forecast on which the spending is based was utilized. For event and product level activities, estimates based on historical information were utilized, where possible. If absent, historical information estimates from people who perform the activities were used.
4. Volume assumption—Logic Level S per planning forecast.
5. Historical yields were used in determining manufactured product costs.

Costs were determined for the 85 key and significant activities identified as part of the activity analysis. The ten highest cost activities accounted for 69% of Logic Level S department overhead spending. Cost per unit of output of each activity was determined by dividing the dollar amount spent on the activity by the total estimated activity output expected for the period of time. The resulting per unit activity costs are documented in the costed Bill of Activities (primary deliverable). Costed activities were also grouped by activity level—unit, batch/lot, product, or event related. The percentage of total for each level was as follows:

	Percentage of Total
Unit	65%
Batch/Lot	5%
Product	16%
Event	14%
Total	100%

Costs were also determined for four high-volume parts selected for the purpose of tracing activity costs to products. Two standard and two custom products were selected. In each case, ABM product cost was lower than the current standard cost. Percentage differences were as follows:

	Percentage of Differences
Standard part 1	7%
Standard part 2	17%
Custom part 1	13%
Custom part 2	21%

A more detailed analysis by activity by manufacturing operation also indicated large discrepancies in both directions at the individual operation level. Comparisons of actual cost to standard cost at other than a macrolevel were difficult due to the outdated standards (2+ years old) and the dramatic change in the MIL/AERO cost structure due to downsizing and reduction efforts previously undertaken.

Observation and learning (step 6)

One purpose of the ABM product costing effort was to gain experience and knowledge that could be applied in future initiatives. Lessons learned include the following:

1. Select a project scope where spending and cost information is readily available. Cost and spending information related to Logic Level S products was not readily available. Accordingly, additional effort was required to isolate Logic Level spending, which entailed assumptions/estimates that decreased the accuracy of the result.
2. Select areas of the business which are relatively stable. Because of reorganizations and changes in MIL/AERO, activities and costs were changing, reflecting the downsizing of the operation. This state of change made the identification and costing of activities difficult.
3. Utilize existing software models for activity costing, if possible. A large part of the effort was directed toward the development of a model to calculate process/product cost. Future efforts should include a step to determine if suitable models exist (internal or external) that could be utilized. If models do not exist, the extra effort necessary to consolidate and report the data must be comprehended and included in the plan.
4. Employ appropriate expertise. The engagement of recognized ABC experts greatly reduced the cycle time and enhanced the results of this costing project.

The Current Situation

Actions taken at the completion of implementation included the following:

1. Refine product/process costing to more accurately comprehend both on-site and corporate allocations.
2. Use the product cost information for the purposes intended.
3. Perform additional analysis of activities with the objective of providing management and teams with information such as cost drivers and performance measures that would help enable cost improvement efforts.
4. Implement an ongoing management reporting system to capture activity information on a regular basis.

SEMATECH

SEMATECH is a not-for-profit research consortium of U.S. semiconductor manufacturers. Founded in 1986, its mission is to solve the technical challenges required to keep the United States number one in the global semiconductor industry. Member companies include AT&T, IBM, Hewlett Packard, Motorola, Rockwell International and the United States Department of Defense. Based in Austin, Texas, SEMATECH employs approximately 600 people (which includes representatives of member companies) under an annual budget of $180 million which includes state-of-the-art wafer fabrication facilities. The SEMATECH Corporate objectives include:

1. Provide member companies with the lowest cost production capability for quality semiconductor products. Reduce or eliminate the rate of increase of capital costs per unit of output despite increasing product complexity.

2. Ensure access to a competitive supplier infrastructure capable of meeting the member companies' requirements for selected key equipment, materials, models, simulation tools, and manufacturing systems.

3. Provide cost-effective, flexible factory capabilities that can respond to process/product changes with first-pass success.

4. Provide solutions to the semiconductor industry for environment, safety, and health (ESH) conscious manufacturing.

5. Provide member companies with significant return on investment.

6. Champion the national semiconductor technology roadmaps and work with the government to implement timely improvements in semiconductor technology. Cooperate with all organizations involved in semiconductor R&D to develop a research infrastructure necessary to sustain U.S. leadership in semiconductor technology.

7. Maintain open forums for effective communications, collaboration, and consensus building within the SEMATECH community.

SEMATECH is an excellent example of a bottom-up grassroots implementation effort. A spark of interest was ignited when a member of SEMATECH's financial staff attended a public ABM seminar in late 1992. Recognizing the potential value of ABM to SEMATECH and knowledge of member companies' interest led this individual to request a team charter from SEMATECH's Total Quality Steering Committee. The team charter requested resources to use ABM to identify activities, inputs, outputs, cost drivers, and performance measures and to validate resources for two SEMATECH projects and the manufacturing support area. Nine team members were requested, each contributing 15% of their time to this implementation effort. Although the request was approved in early January 1993, the actual effort did not commence until mid-April and was completed about two months later. The initial project objectives and the boundaries and constraints agreed to by the team and the Steering Committee were as follows:

Project Objectives
- Identify 70% of the key and significant activities within the two projects and manufacturing support.
- Identify 60% of the costs and their drivers.
- Define the triggers (inputs) and output measures for the associated activities.
- Prioritize the activities for improvement.
- Provide management with recommendations for change with corresponding impacts on cost.
- Determine applicability and obtain management support for using ABM in other areas of SEMATECH.

Boundaries and Constraints
- Have a customer defined.
- Relate project to an organizational goal.
- Do not conflict with other improvement activities.
- Focus on value to the customer (member companies).
- Pick a project with maximum impact.

Because the implementation was relatively simple, covering the activities of 35 people involved in two SEMATECH projects (FIT and ESO) and the manufacturing support area (MS), the implementation plan was concise and consisted only of milestone completion dates for each of the three areas. The eight-step milestone project plan is set forth as follows:

Milestone	Overall Project	FIT	MS	ESO
1. Project plan and training complete	4/9/93			
2. Validate activities with project managers		4/22/93	5/13/93	5/27/93
Validate activities input/output				
3. Determine external triggers		4/29/93	5/20/93	6/3/93
Determine customers/ dependencies				
Determine performance measures				
4. Cost drivers for activities		5/7/93	5/21/93	6/10/93
Costing the activities				
Classification of activities				
Prepare bill of activities				
5. Midpoint report preparation	5/20/93			
6. Submit midpoint reports to management	5/27/93			
7. Final reports on projects completed		5/14/93	5/25/93	6/17/93
8. Final report validation and preparation	6/18/93			

The success of this initial work led to similar efforts in several additional departments and areas of the organization, the most significant of which was the Advanced Tool Development Facility (ATDF), which consumed about 10% of SEMATECH resources and employed 130 people. That effort commenced in early August 1993 and was completed by mid-October 1993.

In terms of people, approach, responsibilities, time lines, requirements, and deliverables, this ATDF effort was very similar to the MIL/AERO project at National Semiconductor, and deployment, except for the technical problems, was almost identical. Because National Semiconductor is one of the SEMATECH member companies, there was a willingness to share experiences and implementation knowledge. One difference was the purpose/objective for each of the projects. National Semiconductor was interested in accurate product cost for product decisions. SEMA-TECH does not sell wafers, so the objectives and purposes were different and were stated as follows:

♦ Monitor and control processes to improve productivity and efficiency.

♦ Determine priorities for manufacturing.

♦ Establish service pricing.

♦ Make decisions on products/services that may be offered for sale outside SEMATECH.

This additional ABM effort was also successful, and during the last part of 1993 and all of 1994, additional areas and departments began ABM initiatives. By mid-1995, 80% of the key and significant activities for SEMATECH had been defined and analyzed. In addition to its own internal efforts, SEMATECH has been a catalyst to ABM implementation in the semiconductor industry. Through SEMATECH's leadership, several member company ABM workshops have been conducted, which has been helpful in the transfer of knowledge.

The Current Situation

The ABM effort at SEMATECH is an example of a grass roots effort that succeeded. ABM is now a cornerstone of quality improvement initiatives and linked to all major SEMATECH initiatives. It also provides an example of what one person can do when he or she puts his or her mind to it. Led by Ashok Vadgama, the effort was largely successful because of his tenacity.

The overall ABM implementation plan or vision for 1995 was as follows:

1. Activity-based costing for the rest of SEMATECH—institutionalize by December 1995.

2. Performance-based activity accounting system in place to show the following:

   Linkage between budget and actual

   Inputs/Outputs

   Cost drivers

   Links to existing internal measurement systems

   Reconcile traditional versus ABC

As if, what if, decisions

Performance matrix

Cost per milestones, goals

3. Member company task force meetings, every three months, and workshops, twice a year.

4. Linkage to SEMI/SEMATECH members. SEMI/SEMATECH members represent equipment suppliers.

5. Transfer of knowledge to member/supplier companies.

6. Business process relationship map for major business process in SEMATECH.

7. Integrated performance measuring (philosophy of total quality combined within the company rather than a separate department).

8. Monitor and track activity performance.

9. Training for SEMATECH employees.

10. Identify/advise management on opportunities for improvement.

UNION PACIFIC RESOURCES CORPORATION

Union Pacific Resources is a part of Union Pacific Corporation and is responsible for its oil and gas drilling and production operations in North America. Union Pacific Resources' ABM project was initiated in September 1993 to improve internal customer service and to meet the customer needs of the accounting and information services departments. An ABM core implementation team was formed from members of both departments. The core team was given the responsibility to successfully implement ABM and to select the outside resources to support them in their efforts. The implementation effort was initiated with project planning on October 18, 1993 and formally kicked off on November 3, 1993 with an employees meeting of all accounting and information services personnel (approximately 200 people). The data gathering and workshop portion of the implementation effort was completed December 16, 1993. The final report summarizing work performed and results obtained was completed December 23, 1993.

Union Pacific Resources utilized an accelerated form of ABM known as FastTrack ABM. FastTrack ABM is a unique approach to ABM that combines group techniques, process mapping, and activity costing to shorten the implementation effort from months to weeks and involves a concentrated effort over a short period of time.

The purpose of the effort was as follows:

1. To stick a stake in the ground that represented current cost performance of activities and services provided to operating personnel.

2. Identify and set goals and opportunities for improvement that could be implemented in 1994.

3. To establish an ongoing reporting system so that accounting and information services managers are provided with activity-based cost and performance information on a regular basis.

The expected result of this effort was to direct the accounting and information services department's focus in two areas:

♦ Customer focus:

Implementing a more meaningful method for communicating the cost of services to internal customers

Providing customers with an improved understanding of accounting and information services activities and how customers can help reduce the cost of those activities

Identifying activities that add no value to achieve strategic objectives

♦ Improvement focus. To support ongoing continuous improvement efforts in accounting and information services by providing the following:

A sound baseline for understanding current activities and their costs

Performance measurements that focus on key activities and motivate continuous improvement

Providing management with a list of improvement opportunities for streamlining the accounting and information services areas

Actions necessary to effect improvement

Objectives and Scope of Effort

All departments, functions, and responsibilities of the accounting and information services departments were included. The objectives of the ABM initiative was to implement an ongoing reporting system that would meet Union Pacific Resources' needs by providing the following:

♦ An improved understanding of the cost of activities and outputs within the accounting and information services departments.

♦ Identification of non-value-added activities.

♦ Prioritizing opportunities for improving activities and processes.

♦ Development of improved performance measurements and reporting capabilities.

Deliverables from this project include the following:

♦ An activity dictionary that included each of the key and significant activities identified.

♦ Costing of those activities and outputs such as to enable more accurately communicating the cost of products/services to internal customers.

♦ An ongoing ABM data analysis system.

♦ Process maps for activities within the accounting and information services functions.

♦ Key performance measurements and cost drivers for each area.

♦ A list of opportunities to improve the activities and processes.

♦ A group of Union Pacific team members trained in ABM concepts, tools, and techniques.

♦ A final report that documented the results of the project effort.

Implementation and Deployment

The project was conducted using the FastTrack ABM approach and utilized teams from each functional area working in a fast-paced workshop environment to do the following:

♦ Define departmental outputs (services).

♦ Identify key and significant activities required to produce those services.

♦ Trace resource cost to the activities and services.

♦ Develop process maps.

♦ Identify opportunities for improvement.

♦ Develop performance measurements.

A core team of 11 members was assigned to oversee the project and to develop specific expertise in ABM. The core team also played a key role in facilitating work sessions and coordinating data entry and report development. Members of this team devoted an average of about 50% of their time to the project throughout its duration. The total duration of the project was about six working weeks, from November 3 through December 23.

Eleven teams were formed to participate in FastTrack ABM workshops conducted for the 11 major areas of Union Pacific Resources' accounting and information services functions. The workshops generally consisted of five half-day sessions. In larger or more complex areas, additional days were required, while in some of the smaller areas only two or three half-day sessions were necessary to complete the analysis.

Each team summarized the result of their efforts in a report that contained the following areas:

♦ Executive summary.

♦ Key and significant activities.

♦ Performance measures.

♦ Non-value-added analysis.

♦ Improvement opportunities.

♦ Action plan.

♦ Appendix (containing the activity dictionary and process maps for each of the activities identified).

Key Findings

Key findings and actions included the following:

1. Eighty-one key and significant activities were identified for the accounting department; 56 for information services. The ten highest cost activities accounted for 46% and 30% of total annual costs for the accounting and information services departments, respectively.

2. A complete value-added analysis was performed on all 81 activities of the accounting department. This analysis was performed in two stages:

A. Each activity was reviewed and analyzed from a yes/no perspective. The activity was or was not value added. Non-value-added activities accounted for 6% of cost.

B. For each significant valued-added activity, additional analysis was performed to determine the extent of significant non-value-added tasks associated with the value-added activity. Cost was determined for many of these non-value-added tasks and represented about 20% of total spending.

3. The non-value-added analysis for information services identified non-value-added activities that represented 21% of total cost.

4. Action plans to address the opportunities for improvement were prepared for each of the 11 individual groups/teams. These action plans were fairly general and were prepared at a high level. While sufficient for initial efforts, additional refinement and details were required.

5. For those improvement opportunities that involved the elimination of work performed, absent further actions, the result could be the creation of excess capacity. In order for these opportunities to have impact on the bottom line, this capacity must be redeployed and assigned to activities that create value.

The Current Situation

Activity performance for each of the 11 areas of accounting and information services continues to be reviewed on a quarterly basis with management. Since 1993, several additional support departments of Union Pacific Resources have undertaken ABM in their respective area of responsibility. In 1996, the company intends to begin using ABM in the operations area.

The ABM implementation at Union Pacific Resources is a good example of how support departments of large companies often use ABM. More frequently than ever, organizations are requiring their support departments to determine the cost of services provided and to take aggressive actions to improve activity performance. This ABM implementation also illustrates the detail at which activities are often defined (137 activities were specified for accounting and information systems), when the objective is to use the information for process improvement.

SHAFFER

Shaffer was a manufacturing company in the oil service industry and was a division of a Fortune 500 company. Their customers were oil company and independent oil and gas drilling operators. Major products were capital equipment items used in oil drilling operations. In 1990, revenues were about $50 million, and the company employed 350 people.

At its peak in 1982, Shaffer revenues were over $200 million. However, like every company in the oil service industry, revenues and employment had declined significantly since the high of 1982, and Shaffer was only marginally profitable in 1990.

Activity-based cost management (at that time, the acronym was ABCM) was introduced to Shaffer by a person assigned the task of identifying cost improvement opportunities at Shaffer. This ABCM champion made a recommendation to management that ABCM concepts and principles would be beneficial to the company and scheduled an expert to conduct an in-house seminar on ABCM for middle managers. Several months later, the company committed to a two-phase, seven-month implementation effort. Phase I was a one-month overall assessment of current operations to define business processes and key activities, provide estimates of annual cost, and select one of those business processes for detail review and analysis. Phase II was directed toward the selected business process and its key and significant activities to determine costs, value versus nonvalue added, productivity measures, and cost drivers. The purpose was to make specific recommendations for management action to eliminate or reduce non-value-added activities and waste. The intention was to redeploy resources from non-value-added activities to productive and beneficial work.

To kick off this phase I effort, the president of Shaffer sent a letter to all key managers in the organization. This letter was well written and received. The body of the letter, absent references to specific names of people, is reproduced in Exhibit 9–1. This was a good example of an internal communication to inform people about the kick off of ABM implementation effort. The results of the phase I effort were as follows:

1. Business process relationship map completed. The business process relationship map identified seven business processes (see Exhibit 9–2).

Exhibit 9–1. ABM Implementation—Communications Letter

TO:	All Managers
FROM:	The President
SUBJECT:	Improving Productivity and Efficiency

Because of the pressures we face to be profitable in the short term, we can sometimes lose sight of the longer-term things we need to do to build strength in our company. Strength comes from serving customers in an efficient and productive way. We all have customers . . . whether it's the outside customer who uses our products and services or the inside customer who used the services of others as the resource to accomplish their objectives. We all rely on one another.

Improving long-term productivity and efficiency is a goal we have for our company. To that end, we have established a project and earmarked resources to accomplish this goal. The purpose of the project is to identify and eliminate work that doesn't need to be done so that we can use this resource to do the things that matter and which will improve productivity and efficiency. We'll call these improvements operations savings, and in most cases these savings will not result in immediate cost reduction. Rather, we want long-term cost improvement that results from being productive and efficient by spending time on the things that matter and doing away with non-essential work.

The project will be spearheaded using the principals and methods of Activity-Based Cost Management. Simply stated, ABCM is the collection of cost and operation information about the activities of the business—what our people and machines actually do every day. ABCM provides an organized way for us to look at the effectiveness and efficiency of our organization and to determine the cause of cost.

A project team, lead by _____ , will be established for this company-wide effort. The team will report to the task fore committee of _____ , _____ , _____ . Team members will be asked to devote ____% of their effort to the project. In addition, we have contracted with an outside consultant, _____ , to assist and guide in project implementation. _____ will bring some outside expertise and thinking to the project. This initial project will last seven months. We will evaluate the overall results and benefits received, as the project progresses.

As management, we must be committed to building strength in the organization longer-term, by improving productivity and efficiency. We must be willing to commit today's hard earned dollars to improve operations longer-term. As managers we have no choice, if we intend to compete efficiently in our markets. I urge you to support the project and the project team, to think about what we're all doing, and how it could be done better.

Exhibit 9–2. Business Process Relationship Map—Shaffer

SUMMARY OF CRITICAL BUSINESS PROCESSES

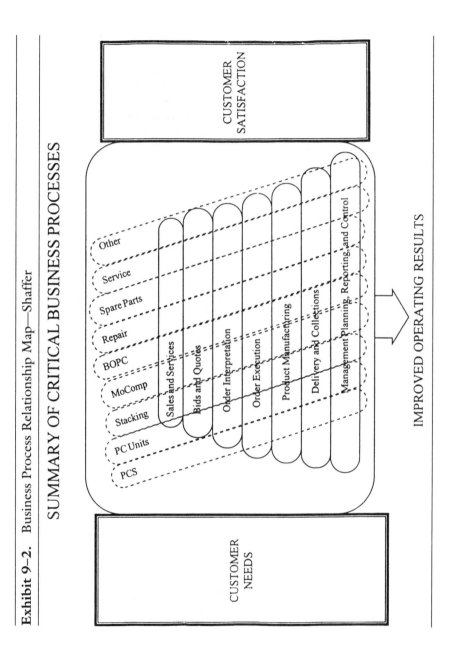

The horizontal bars that start with sales and service and end with management planning, reporting, and control represented the business processes, as defined by Shaffer. The business processes were arranged in sequential order from top to bottom and shown in a way to indicate that much of the work was performed simultaneously. The vertical bars represented the company's individual product lines.

2. Types of costs, key activities, possible measures of efficiency, and cost drivers for each business process were identified.

3. Traditional versus activity-based costs were determined.

4. Recommendation to perform a more rigorous analysis of activities, tasks, and costs associated with one of the business processes.

The phase I implementation at Shaffer, conducted many years ago, was a crude form of the overall assessment we recommend today as part of the ABM implementation. Phase I was a top-down driven look at the organization from the perspective of activities. The assessment was designed to select a piece of the organization for phase II where improvement initiatives would be beneficial and could be completed in three to four months. In making this selection, management had two viable alternatives to consider. One alternative was to perform a more rigorous analysis of activities, tasks, and costs associated with a single business process, or part thereof. The other alternative was to improve all processes for one product. After examining the pros and cons of each alternative, management elected a product approach and chartered a team to establish an ongoing effort to effect operations improvements in its PCS product line and initiated the phase II implementation effort.

In this situation example, ABM drove this organization to eventually implement a TQM initiative. At one point they had completed 30 total quality improvement initiatives when their efforts were overcome by events. Additional reductions in drilling activity led to fewer sales and additional layoffs. The division was sold, and its operations were consolidated with the purchaser. All momentum was lost.

CATERAIR INTERNATIONAL

Caterair International is a privately held company that prepares airline meals and caters commercial aircraft. The company operates over 130 kitchens worldwide, and virtually every airline uses Caterair services on some flights. The main proponent of ABM at Caterair was the director of pricing, based at corporate headquarters. Her interest was in the use of ABM information to negotiate better contracts with airline customers.

In the spring of 1991, representatives of Caterair completed three ABM benchmarking visits. The purpose of these visits was to learn about ABM and identify benefits, if any, to Caterair and to recommend next steps. The results of these visits was documented for management and included the following items contained in the benchmarking report:

1. Activity-based management is being implemented or piloted in each of the three companies visited. Based on these visits and other research, it is apparent that ABM is becoming the leading industry approach to allocating and understanding overhead costs.

2. Activity-based costing is based on the assumption that activities consume costs and that products consume activities. Activity-based management systems focus on what drives the consumption of resources.

3. The TQM and ABM systems are complementary business strategies. Total quality management focuses on process improvement; ABC is a tool to quantify the costs of the process.

4. All the companies interviewed use ABM information as a means to measure performance and the results of process improvements. Changing pricing strategy could be a result of this but was not the driving force. At one company, in particular, operations were demanding ABM information; finance and accounting were not dictating it.

5. Identifying the cost drivers and determining how to track them is one of the challenges of implementing an ABM system.

6. The companies used different approaches to implement ABM. One company paid for consultants to set up a pilot site. Another just attended outside seminars.

In December of 1991, a proposed initiative covering the problem, proposed initiative, and expected benefits, was presented to the quality council seeking a go-ahead for an ABM initiative. The problem was that Caterair did not have an accurate method for tracking costs. The correlation between costs and changes in activity in the kitchen had not been quantified. In addition, few costs performance measures had been developed. The proposed initiative was to develop an ABM system in a pilot kitchen.

The ABM system would track costs by activity and airline, quantify and support the goal of continuous process improvement, provide better performance measures, and identify non-value-added activities. It would also provide better information for bids.

There were several benefits expected from ABM. The first expected benefit was that, by understanding clearly what drives costs, profits would improve. Competitive advantage was expected to be gained. With a better understanding of how costs react to change, there would be a higher confidence in the pricing model and less need to increase costs to cover the unknown. In this business, low cost is a competitive advantage. In addition, implementing ABM was a proactive step for cost management that would be recognized by customers. Customers were requiring more cost information. This information could eventually be used as a marketing tool to demonstrate to customers that procedures and methods are in place to control costs.

Attached to the proposed initiative was a preliminary implementation schedule that requested a 150-person day resource commitment and a seven-month time line for project completion. The quality council approved, as a next step, a training seminar and workshop for key corporate personnel and line operating managers. The purpose of the seminar was twofold:

1. Management level overview of ABM, including definitions, principles, features, uses, application, design, and implementation.
2. To specify on a preliminary basis the major business processes and key activities for a kitchen operation.

Subsequent to the training and workshop, the quality council approved an ABM pilot implementation at their Boston kitchen. The effort commenced in mid-April 1992 and was completed by the end of June. The project objective was to develop and install an ABM system in the Boston kitchen. The project deliverable and final report were to include the following:

♦ Identification of the key and significant activities for the Boston kitchen. Activities identified and documented in an activity dictionary.

♦ Business process relationship map linking activities to business processes.

♦ Comparison of activity-based costs with traditional reporting of costs.

♦ Ranking of activities for improvement.

♦ Summary, observations, conclusions, recommendations, and next steps.

Implementation and Deployment

The initial training and workshop, whose participants included the Boston kitchen manager, was successful in that there was a high level of consensus as to seven business processes that applied to a kitchen operation. These business processes served as the starting point for the implementation. The overall plan of implementation was to establish two teams of three people, whose responsibility was to analyze specific business processes. A third team was responsible for activity/product costing. Three group meetings were held over a 2½-month period, to review the result of work completed. These meetings were attended by Boston operating personnel. A final group meeting was held to discuss overall results and to agree on final recommendations.

The primary data gathering technique for activity analysis was the use of interviews with employees that worked in each of the functional areas of the kitchen. Guidelines used by team members for interviews included the following:

♦ The interview process should be fun.

♦ Meet with managers and supervisors who will participate in the process being reviewed. Provide them with a brief survey, and ask them to think about the questions.

♦ Based on operating personnel's advise, be available to observe and interview at off-hours as needed.

♦ Record the interviews visibly on a flip chart. Remind the people being interviewed that nothing is cast in stone; they can make changes after they have had time to think about the questions.

♦ Avoid using the words rank, cost, or waste during the interview.

The short- and long-term recommendations of the project team were as described in the following.

Short term

The Boston kitchen will use ABM reports starting with August results. These reports will be provided on a weekly basis for four to six weeks. At the end of six weeks, the TQM team will meet and evaluate Boston's experience with ABC. Final recommendations to the quality steering committee were based on this evaluation.

During the six-week evaluation, ABM reports will be compared with traditional cost management reports to determine if the new reports are a better method for understanding cost performance in a kitchen. In addition, Boston will choose an activity for process improvement. By documenting the work flow in this activity, a direction will be set for process improvement. The ABM reports will be used to track this process improvement. Quality measures will be set for the activity to ensure that quality improves as cost decreases.

Long term

The long-term recommendations were as follows:

1. The team agreed upon the need to validate the Boston model. This was not to be undertaken until Boston's six-week pilot was complete. Based on those results, the team will recommend getting additional input on the ABM model developed in Boston. Validation would be obtained by the following:

   ◆ Reviewing the process and activity model in a shop in another region or one shop in each region.

   ◆ Presenting the concept at regional general manager meetings.

2. If ABM is implemented in other kitchens, the team recommends it as a powerful tool to identify and share best practices for activities and processes.

3. Activity-based management information could be used to set internal benchmarks for activities.

4. Using activity-based information to shift the emphasis from kitchens as profit centers to kitchens as cost centers for purposes of evaluating the performance of a kitchen. The general managers would have a tool that would indicate their ability to control costs as they relate to volumes of output for varying activities, as opposed to profit measures (such as sales per man-hour) that are skewed by revenue factors, which are only partially controllable by the general manager.

5. The team recommends that the focus of ABM be for use by the general manager at the shop level.

6. The team identified the potential to use ABM to develop cost structures by airline and also to apply the concepts to corporate overhead functions.

The Current Situation

Almost immediately after this pilot effort was completed, American Airlines initiated changes to airfare structures that ignited a fare war among airline carriers that resulted in selling out virtually every seat on every flight, for the entire summer of 1992. This implementation effort, like Shaffer, was overcome by events, and the recommendations of the project team were never implemented completely. However, not all was lost. The data, analysis, information, and results of the Boston pilot initiative have been instrumental and useful to recently renewed efforts directed toward business process improvement.

As these ten examples illustrate, much can be accomplished with an aggressive ABM implementation effort. From a single department of a Fortune 500 company to the majority of operations for a medium-sized publicly held company to the operations of an entire government agency, each developed and executed an implementation plan that properly balanced the project scope, with the resources required to implement the plan. It is correct to state that none of the foregoing implementations were complete at the end of the initial phase of implementation. Each of these implementations required additional efforts to develop ongoing information and reporting systems and involved additional phases of work to drive the knowledge of key and significant activities to a more detailed level of understanding.

10

Ongoing System Requirements

Most ABM implementations fail to place sufficient emphasis on installing the systems, procedures, and methods necessary to collect and report activity-based information on an ongoing basis. As a result, the systems, procedures, and methods that are installed are often unresponsive to the needs of the users, difficult to update and maintain, and unreliable. The systems and software aspect of the ABM implementation cannot be ignored; in fact it must be emphasized. After all, what is the point of implementing ABM unless it is to report timely, accurate, and relevant ABM information on a continuing basis. Without continuous ABM reporting the ABM implementation is a nonevent.

The reason many organizations place insufficient emphasis on the systems aspect of the ABM implementation can again be traced to its history. Until recently, most ABM implementations were undertaken on a pilot or test basis in parts and pieces of large organizations. Decisions on the software, systems, methods, and procedures were made to address the needs of the pilot effort(s). Few organizations addressed the long-term total ABM information needs of the total organization. That is why we recommend a more total or holistic approach to implementation that includes emphasis on the selection and development of cost-effective ongoing data collection and reporting systems to collect and report ABM data at the level of detail, accuracy, and frequency required by the users of the information.

In this chapter we will review examples of ABM reporting systems to acquaint the reader with the range of ABM systems solutions. This chapter will also discuss the ABM system design considerations, the two stages of system implementation, hardware/software issues, and conclude with a review of the commercially available ABM software and software selection criteria.

EXAMPLES OF ABM REPORTING SYSTEMS

Examples of software and systems that have been developed to collect and report ABM information range from simple spreadsheets updated and maintained by a single person using a PC to fully integrated ABM information warehouses, updated continuously and accessed, on-line, by multilevel people at individual worldwide sites.

Some organizations have developed simple ABM information systems using commercially available spreadsheet software applications like Microsoft's Excel. Spreadsheets are maintained to trace resources (costs) to activities and to trace activity costs to cost objects like products and services. Often the spreadsheets are linked together and are very elaborate in their ability to download and extract data from other systems. These homegrown systems work very nicely in the initial and analysis stage of the ABM implementation but are generally not satisfactory as a long-term solution because the ABM information collected and reported is often limited to cost. Cost drivers, performance measures, and activity outputs are typically not captured or reported.

Some organizations have integrated the cost element of an ABM system directly with the internal accounting and financial systems. In these examples, cost data entering the accounting systems are coded to the specific activities defined and specified in the accounting records. Cost information collected in this manner can be reported through the existing accounting and financial systems. The problem here is the same as for the spreadsheet applications. The ABM information tends to be cost only and the systems are not generally capable of reporting cost drivers, performance measures, or activity outputs.

A significant number of organizations use commercial ABM software to meet their ABM reporting requirements. In general, these systems have been designed to meet the most demanding of ABM applications. They shorten the ABM system development time and are generally efficient and effective for the ongoing collection and reporting of most ABM data.

There are several examples of organizations that have developed and installed ABM systems that are fully integrated and linked with internal financial and operating systems. Not surprisingly, one of those organizations is EDS who developed their ABM system using a relational database at its Strategic Support Unit (SSU). The SSU is comprised of large data processing centers located worldwide. Combined, the SSU is responsible for costs of $1.5 billion, of which 80% is included in the ABM information reporting system.

The ABM initiative at EDS is focused in two areas. The first area includes primary ABM applications of process improvement, cost reduction, performance measurement, and budgeting, directed toward providing ABM information to drive and support improvement initiatives. The second area of focus is on service cost and cost estimation. The detail required by operating personnel to effect process improvement and measurement in the support areas required capturing and reporting data on approximately 1,600 activities. To meet these operational requirements, EDS designed, developed, and installed a fully integrated (internal reporting and operating systems) ABM information system that is updated continuously.

The base system, or ABM information warehouse, is a relational database running in a client server on-line environment with multiplatform access by Macintosh, DOS/Windows, and UNIX. Automated interfaces between the general ledger, equipment/volume tracking, and human resources systems feed and update the relational database continuously. The relational database provides on-line reporting options for products (services), quality, cost drivers, processes (activity), and value added. The systems and systems interfaces were developed so that general ledger cost data and ABM cost data always agreed. At EDS, absent agreement, the ABM data would lose credibility.

ABM information is accessible on-line to over 500 users at 70 EDS worldwide sites. Systems users include corporate officers, directors, managers, supervisors, team leaders, and employees involved in process improvement teams.

As these examples were intended to illustrate, there are many alternatives to the design and installation of the ongoing ABM information system. Many of the alternatives will be driven by the purpose and use of the activity-based information. A system, like the one developed by EDS, would not be useful in the situation where the purpose and intent of the system was to calculate true product/service cost on an annual basis. In designing the ABM information system, much needs to be taken into account.

STAGES OF IMPLEMENTATION

There are two stages to implementing ongoing ABM information systems. Stage 1 involves establishing the base set of procedures, systems, and methods for collecting information. Stage 2 relates to ongoing system maintenance requirements.

Under stage 1, procedures, systems, and methods needed for ongoing reporting are implemented. This often involves creating procedures to collect data for the first time, as well as redirecting information and data from existing sources. Stage 1 requires extensive training of personnel in the use of ABM. Due dates and implementation schedules should be established, and the quality requirements expected of data entering the system should be standardized.

The stage 1 ABM information system is complete when the following are achieved:

1. The collection and reporting of activity information for each activity contained in the activity dictionary is provided in the required format of the user, at the frequency desired.

2. Management is satisfied that product/service cost is properly calculated and that the information is provided at the frequency intended.

Stage 2 involves the ongoing maintenance of the system. By definition, stage 2 is never completed because activities change over time. Since activities are the basis of the ABM system, it must be updated to reflect those changes. If estimates are used, they should be replaced with actual data. Activity-based management system improvements can be made by identifying more accurate activity and resource drivers. New products will also have to be costed. Performance measures may change.

SYSTEM DESIGN CONSIDERATIONS

The first and foremost consideration in the design of the ABM information system is its purpose and use. The system must be designed to meet the needs and requirements of the organization. If the organization has developed an overall ABM implementation plan, as recommended, then the purpose and use of the system would be adequately documented. If not, then this work must be completed and documented as the basic framework for the design of the system.

The purpose and use of ABM will drive both the amount of information that must be collected and the detail to which it must be obtained. In general, ABM applications that are process and performance related like process improvement, re-engineering, project management, activity performance, and benchmarking require more detail and frequency of reporting than those decision-related applications like product costing, capital justification, and target costing (see Exhibit 2–2, ABM Value Cycle).

In a product or service cost application, the minimum base information that must be collected on a forward-looking basis for a specified period of time (i.e., month, quarter, annual) includes the following:

◆ Actual resources expanded.

◆ How people spent their time on activities.

◆ How machine time was spent on activities.

◆ How facilities were used on activities.

◆ How other costs were traced to activities.

◆ Counts of activity outputs.

◆ How activity outputs were consumed by the cost objects identified.

In addition to this minimum base information requirement for product/service costing, counts and measures of activity performance, cost drivers, and benchmarks are often required for process improvement related applications.

In addition to purpose and use, there are many other considerations in designing the ongoing ABM reporting system. These design considerations include accuracy, frequency of update, and relevance.

Accuracy

The level of accuracy required by the ABM information system is a key design consideration. The accuracy of the activity-based information system is dependent on the accuracy of the data entering the system. Traditional cost data are often plagued by allocations, misapplied costs, assumptions, and incorrect coding such that the data are unreliable. Data from other operating systems can be equally unreliable. Accuracy, as it relates to the existing operating environment, must be assessed. High levels of accuracy require fact-based, reliable data.

The selection and use of activity and resource drivers will also affect system accuracy. Activity and resource drivers are often estimates. A common resource driver for tracing salary/wage costs to activities are estimates made by people on how they spend their time. For many ABM implementations, resource drivers are developed based on interviews with selected people and resultant percentages applied to the employee base. Accuracy is an issue when using interviews of personnel to determine how they spend their time on various activities. This is because the way people actually spend their time is different than the way they think they spend it.

That is why in some organizations, where high levels of accuracy are required, people provide regular updates on how they spend their time, by activity. There is generally a high level of resistance when white-collar workers are asked to keep track of their time. However, this resistance may be overcome when three points are considered:

♦ In many companies, the total cost of employees (salary, fringe benefits, and items like supplies, travel, and meals, which are consumed by individual employees) can represent 60% or more of the total cost structure of the organization. There are very few companies where the total cost of employees is insignificant. It is reasonable to monitor this significant cost and to direct this resource toward activities that add value to the organization.

♦ Any good time management course advises that, to improve the use of an individual's time, a time log should be kept to learn exactly how time is spent. To improve time management for an entire organization, managers should do for the organization what is done for the individual—monitor how time is spent and what it is spent on.

♦ With current information technology, the effort to collect these data should not be cumbersome. Systems are in place today that require less than one minute for a user to record time by activity once a week.

For many organizations, resource drivers for people, machines, and facility costs will account for 80 to 90% of total cost (excluding raw material purchases). The use of facilities and machines often tends to remain static over time (i.e., the resource drivers do not change materially from period to period). Therefore, if the initial ABM analysis is adequate, these drivers should be reasonably accurate going forward.

Frequency of Update

Some organizations view ABM as a strategic tool only. Activity-based information is updated and used annually to set goals, to align resources, for capital appropriation, and for product/service related decisions of mix, pricing, and capacity. Other organizations see the strategic value of ABM information and supplement this use with quarterly updates as a way to monitor activity performance and product/service cost. Still other organizations use ABM information operationally, where activities and products/services are costed on a monthly basis for management review. Finally, for certain activities, real-time activity-based measures may be required where high-volume activities are monitored on an hourly, daily, or weekly basis.

The frequency of distribution and update is largely a function of the system's purpose and use. It would not be unusual to report cost and performance measurements on an hourly basis for some activities yet on a quarterly basis for others. The reporting of activity performance on both an hourly and a quarterly basis could exist within the system framework, assuming that activity performance is measured and reported to a line manager hourly and summarized in a quarterly report to top management. Whether reported on an hourly, monthly, or quarterly basis, the activity is the same—only the period of performance varies.

The design considerations of accuracy and the frequency of update trade off are a function of its purpose and use. Establishing a detailed labor reporting system to track people's time would not make sense if the information was only required on an annual basis. Conversely, using an estimate of how people spend their time as a resource driver would be dangerous if not updated or if used to report monthly activity results.

Relevance

For a new ABM information system to be useful, its focus must be on the important aspects of the business, at a level relevant to improvement efforts and for decision making. A cornerstone of an effective ABM information system is the avoidance of complexity whenever possible. The simpler a procedure is, the easier it is to implement and the greater support it provides management. Designers of an ABM system can follow the lead of their manufacturing counterparts, the designers of machinery. Machinery designers have learned that complex designs lead to complex repair problems and difficult modifications. Complexity can come in little doses, as when using two different kinds of fasteners in a product when one kind would do the job. Complexity adds cost, does not improve functionality, and must constantly be designed out of products and services.

There is no reason to believe that it would be different for designers of ABM systems. Designing an ABM system with a high degree of complexity means that management will be giving up future flexibility and guaranteeing that modifications, improvements, and changes will be difficult and costly. A basic rule to follow when designing a new system is as follows: If the users of the output are unable to understand the system's basic features and functions, then the system is too complex.

Activity-based management information systems should be designed so that users can compare relevant internal costs and performance measures of activities with externally driven targets. Activity-based system designers should anticipate and plan to compare internal cost and measurements with external standards and requirements. Management can then set standards or highlight performance gaps for a particular activity or business process. Design specifications should take into account such techniques as benchmarking, best practices, and target costing.

HARDWARE AND SOFTWARE ISSUES

The key issue when examining hardware and software is whether to implement the ABM system off-line through a stand-alone (or networked) personal computer or to integrate the system on-line as part of the existing financial and operation systems. Most organizations, at least initially, would be better served if they implemented an ABM system on a stand-alone basis using activity-based software currently offered in the marketplace. This approach enables the designers to gain hands-on experience and knowledge about activity management without committing the organization to a major change of systems.

Many organizations use these commercial activity-based software packages for their ongoing reporting and system requirements. These programs are available from a number of organizations. Each of these software packages are similar in that they accept general ledger cost and operational data and reformat and report the cost information in activity format based on the assumptions (resource and activity drivers) specified in the system.

There are ten major activity-based software packages currently available in the marketplace. They can be grouped into two categories: those developed and sold by independent software vendors and those developed or supported by one of the big six public accounting firms. These are outlined in the following:

Independents

♦ NetProphet II (Sapling Software).

♦ Easy ABC Plus/OROS (ABC Technologies).

♦ DaCapo Process Manager (ABM-I).

♦ CMS-PC (ICMS).

♦ CASSO (Automation Consulting).

♦ HyperABC (Armstrong Laing).

Big-Six Public Accounting Firms

♦ TR/ACM (Deloitte & Touche).

♦ Activa (Price Waterhouse).

♦ Profit Manager Plus 3 (KPMG Peat Marwick).

♦ ABCost Manager (Cooper & Lybrand)

NetProphet II (Sapling Software)

NetProphet II is cost management software that combines ABC and process analysis using a graphic user interface. The basic features include the ability to create a model of the process being analyzed, verify and validate the model that has been built, play what are called scenarios, and generate reports. Building a model using NetProphet II involves three steps: entering preliminary data, entering boxes and linking them together, and verifying the model.

Once a model has been verified and validated, "scenarios" can be run, which is the primary purpose of NetProphet II. Scenarios are essentially what-if calculations. They allow a user to make changes to the data and to see the impact on operational flow, revenues, and costs. This enables a user to immediately see the consequence of changes in policies, product demand levels, staffing, resources, or equipment.

The reporting feature of NetProphet II allows a user to generate reports concerning the operational and financial results of scenarios or to provide information about the models created. These reports can be viewed on the screen, printed, or saved to disk. In summary, NetProphet II offers the ability to trace costs from resources to activities, to subsequent related activities, and finally, to the cost object, which may or may not be a product/service.

EasyABC/OROS (ABC Technologies, Inc.)

ABC Technologies, Inc. offers three versions of its software to suit a variety of markets. EasyABC Quick is offered for educational purposes, EasyABC Plus for stand alone ABM business applications, and OROS for a multiuser full production system.

EasyABC Plus uses a two-stage allocation method similar in approach to that included in the CAM-I model. EasyABC Plus (which also provides a graphic user interface) includes three modules: a resource module, an activity module, and a cost object module. Each module is hierarchical. The modules are made up of components called centers and accounts, activities, or cost objects. The resource module contains the expenses that are to be traced to activities.

The activity module is probably the most critical module for activity-based cost analysis. In this module, a user organizes the activities that are consumed by products. Activities can be grouped into activity centers, which might be a department. The final module is the cost object module. In this module, users define the cost objects to which they want to trace costs. EasyABC Plus allows for flexibility in defining what a cost object is. For example, a cost object might be a product, a customer, a product line, a service, or any combination of these.

After an activity-based costing model has been built, cost data and the driver data for the period may be entered, after which the actual cost allocations can be performed. EasyABC Plus provides users the ability to generate a variety of standard reports based on data tables. These reports include the following:

◆ Bill of activities.

◆ Bill of costs.

◆ Attribute costing.

◆ Performance measure for each center, account, or entered cost element. (These performance measures are helpful in benchmarking and in evaluating product quality, employee productivity, and cycle time.)

OROS is a Windows-based client server application. It includes a LAN-based framework, free-form report generator, and a direct link to company databases, in addition to the EasyABC Plus capabilities.

CMS-PC (ICMS)

CMS-PC was developed by Integrated Cost Management Systems, based in Arlington, Texas. The software package is spreadsheet based and requires six screens for data entry. CMS-PC uses menus that are designed to guide users through the software. The software consists of the following integrated modules: account analysis, activity analysis, activity accounting, ABC product costing and advanced ABM.

The account analysis module is an importing system designed to help users download general ledger data. The activity analysis module helps users define activities and business processes. Each activity is assigned an output measure to represent the number of times an activity occurs over a particular period. An activity dictionary built into CMS-PC helps users define activities and attributes.

The activity accounting module is based on the principle that activities consume costs. This module traces costs from the general ledger to the activities in each department. After users enter activity output quantities/measures for each activity, CMS-PC calculates the cost-per-activity output. After working through these three modules, a user has designed the basic framework so that the last modules can be implemented.

The fourth module, ABC product costing, is based on the principle that products consume the outputs of activities. A bill of activities is used to determine the costs of products, services, and processes. The ABC product cost is determined by multiplying the cost of each activity output by the quantity of activity outputs consumed by a product or component. The final module, advanced ABM, provides users with activity and process cost information. These are built-in reports and graphs, such as "Value vs. Non-Value-Added Analysis," "Cost of Quality," and "Benchmark Analysis." Users can also create custom reports using a built-in query function.

CASSO (Automation Consulting)

Cost Accounting System for Service Organizations (CASSO) is a menu-driven management accounting system that consists of three integrated modules:

- ◆ Costing.
- ◆ Profitability.
- ◆ General ledger (GL) interface.

The costing module allows users to analyze costs using the standard ABC approach. Users are easily able to define the products (e.g., services or customers), areas (e.g., work units, cost centers, or departments), and activities that they want to track. This module allows development of monthly standards. The profitability module lets users allocate revenues and determines the profitability of their products and areas. As with the costing module, users can define their standards of revenue, enter their actuals, and compute the revenue variances.

The GL interface module automates the transfer of budget and actual dollars from the GL directly into both the costing and profitability modules without additional data entry; it also provides a complete audit trail. A GL account can be mapped to multiple line items by percentages, or multiple GL accounts can be mapped to the same line item. Thus, users have the flexibility they need to maneuver their GL amount to the line items that best allows them to analyze their costs/profits.

The CASSO provides an activity-based method to analyze cost, allocate revenues, and determine the profitability of products. By interfacing with the GL, CASSO ensures the integrity of the data by reducing the volume of data entry required and providing an easy method to balance back to the GL.

HyperABC

HyperABC is designed for companies that want to integrate ABC/ABM into their regular management reporting process and want regular production reporting. The product breaks down into three main functional areas:

1. HyperPort (an electronic data-capture facility).

2. HyperABC the engine (which breaks down into four stages in which ABC information appears in a series of tables having predefined relationships that model the ABC process).

3. HyperLink (a dynamic reporting facility with links to Microsoft Excel, Lotus 1-2-3, and other executive information system software).

Key features include intelligent electronic update facility, easy-to-use interface with "point and click" facility for creating and running models, table-based system with ABC relationships predefined, and automatic validation and reconciliation to source data before calculation.

DaCapo Process Manager

DaCapo Process Manager operates in a Windows environment and can be used on a single PC or in a network. The package has two modules: organization and process. The organization module contains all the steps required to develop a cost accounting system.

From the general ledger, accounts are assigned to natural expense categories (e.g., people, equipment, and facilities). Resources are the key to the cost allocation system, because resources and the associated activities consume expenses. Costs are rolled up from the ledger accounts into resources or cost pools and are associated with user-defined activities.

TR/ACM (Deloitte & Touche)

TR/ACM was developed using a FoxPro database platform to support Deloitte & Touche's strategic cost management (SCM) consulting engagements. The purpose of SCM is to improve and sustain the performance of an organization through the analysis and management of activity-driven resources. The software allows a user to understand the company's basic cost structure and to simulate cost centers. TR/ACM is a single-module software package with a menu system closely linked to Deloitte & Touche's engagement methodology. The main menu offers six basic choices for set-up, libraries, interview, tracing, reporting, and utilities.

ACTIVA (Price Waterhouse)

ACTIVA is a menu-driven activity-based cost modeling and analysis tool. It consists of integrated modules that form a complete package for performing activity-based analysis. These modules are structured as a series of step-by-step operations. ACTIVA controls the sequence of steps and guides the user through each module. The software is designed to help the user see the transition from a traditional accounting system to one that is activity based.

ACTIVA is the only software package built on the UNIX operating system and utilizes an Oracle 7 relational database. It uses a Windows Graphic User Interface to make data entry and analysis more user-friendly. It is a client-server application portable to all platforms supporting UNIX.

Profit Manager Series (KPMG Peat Marwick)

Profit Manager is the foundation of the Peat Marwick Activity-Based Management model. Profit Manager offers up to a ten-level resources structure to accommodate deep general ledger charts of accounts. Resources are driven to activities with resource drivers. Activities are categorized as direct or indirect. Unit-, batch-, and product-sustaining activities are direct, while facility-related and administrative activities are indirect. Indirect activities are driven to other indirect or direct activities, also by use of resource drivers. This feature allows an unlimited number of levels in resource assignment to activities. Location drivers pull activities into user-defined centers; activity drivers pull resources out of centers to products or components. Profit Manager, which uses menus, allows users to define activity attributes and field names. It has a report writer for lists and reports; it also has graphics capabilities.

ABCost Manager (Cooper & Lybrand)

ABCost Manager is a costing and value analysis software package developed by Cooper & Lybrand to support its ABC consulting engagements. ABCost Manager helps a firm develop a business model of the resources used to develop, produce, and sell products and or services. ABCost Manager is menu-driven. There are no separate modules; all features are built around a relational database.

There is an add-on module, BEST, that allows budgeting, estimation, simulation, and target costing. The Profit Manager series is offered in DOS, Windows, and network versions.

SOFTWARE SELECTION CRITERIA

Criteria to be considered in selecting software includes price because significant differences exist. Available features, product and user support, and ease of use and user interface are additional factors and criteria that must be considered. Available features such as target costing, budgeting, and customer profitability analysis, if important, must be considered in selection. Some products are sold as stand-alone software packages, while others come with consulting services as part of the overall package. The level of support required is a significant factor to software selection.

Another criterion, and perhaps the most important, is the track record of the software vendor to regularly expand and update the application software. The application and use of ABM information has rapidly expanded and will continue to do so. Consideration must be given not only to what is important today but also to what will be important in the future. The software vendor's perceived ability to deliver to future requirements is a significant factor to be considered in selecting commercial ABM system software.

A checklist for evaluating an ABM software application is set forth in Exhibit 10–1. The checklist includes five areas of evaluation: vendor char-

---

Exhibit 10–1. Checklist for Evaluating a Software Package

Vendor Characteristics	**Documentation Provided**
Length of time in business	System flowchart
Publicly or privately held	Logic diagram
Dollar volume of software sales for last financial period	Program listings
	File layout(s)
D & B rating (if available)	Input/output formats
Size of technical staff	Operator manuals
Years of experience	**Conversion Costs**
Equipment capabilities	Additional programs needed to
Language proficiencies	convert/build files
General Characteristics	Conversion of records
How many times it has been sold	Direct clerical effort
Price structure for package	Management involvement
What is included in the price	Education
Restrictions on use/sale of package	**Cost of New System**
	Processing cost
Minimum equipment configuration required	Equipment configuration changes
Language used	Additional peripheral equipment
Estimated run times	Input preparation
1. Program by program	Output handling
2. Total system	Audit and control costs
Estimated life of package	Continuing education (at any and all levels)
	Program modification
	Additional documentation

acteristics, general characteristics, documentation provided, conversion costs, and new system costs. It is presented as a fairly exhaustive list. No attempt has been made to attach weight or significance to one factor over another. This checklist can be used as a starting point, and then cut, pasted, and changed to meet the requirements of the specific evaluation. While not included on the checklist, references from existing users of software should be obtained.

One final point needs to be made on the subject of software selection. In 1991, North Carolina State University conducted a survey to determine the criteria, in order of importance, actually used by individuals responsible for selection of activity-based system software. Weights were assigned to each criterion to reflect its relative importance and was based on the survey responses of about two dozen people. Twenty criteria were identified in the survey. The highest criterion scored 82, the lowest (availability/quality of on-line graphics reporting capabilities) scored 18. The top five criteria, together with weight, are as follows:

Criteria	Weight
Technical knowledge of vendor with respect to ABC	82
Flexibility in handling different methodologies for tracing costs	66
Learning curve	65
Type of interface to present accounting/reporting system	60
Track record of vendor with respect to software upgrades	60

SUMMARY

The more total approach to ABM, as recommended in Chapter 3, requires a cost-effective, ongoing data collection and reporting system. The importance of the ongoing system and its requirements have been frequently ignored or given inadequate attention. The result, too frequently, is a system that is not manageable, predictable, or repeatable. That is one of the reasons that many ABM information systems report only on a quarterly basis. Monthly reporting is not manageable, predictable, or repeatable—only overwhelming.

System design considerations include purpose and use, accuracy, frequency of reporting, and relevance. The key system issue to be addressed is whether to purchase a commercial stand-alone (or networked) PC-based application package or to integrate the system on-line as part of existing financial and operations systems. Excellent commercial activity-based software packages are available in the marketplace. These software packages should meet the requirements of most installations. Even when these commercial systems do not meet the long-term requirements of an individual situation, they are still useful in getting the development of the ongoing reporting system started. The information and data developed are not lost when moved from one system to another.

11

Full Integration

Integrating ABM with the base fabric of existing management practices is necessary to achieve full benefit. Activity-based management cannot be seen as a separate and distinct management initiative. It is not strong enough to survive on its own. The real value and power of ABM comes from the knowledge and information that leads to better decisions and improvement. Full integration is complete when people in the organization embrace activity management, take ownership, and internalize it as a better way of doing business and making decisions.

Full integration does not occur overnight. Fully integrating ABM with current and existing philosophies, cultures, organizational priorities, systems, procedures, attitudes, practices, preferences, and values can take years to complete. Efforts are required to drive activity-based thinking deep into the organization. Efforts must be expended to link and integrate ABM with the base information systems used to run and manage the organization.

Specific efforts are required to integrate and link ABM with existing performance measurement systems, improvement initiatives, compensation and reward systems, value-based management, strategic and operations planning, training and education, management control systems, and core competencies. Each of these specific areas of linkage and integration will be reviewed in this final chapter. As a challenge to the reader, this

193

book will conclude with a review of Best Practices in the installation, application, and use of ABM information systems.

PERFORMANCE MEASUREMENT SYSTEMS

Libraries are filled with books on performance measurement. The subject can become exceedingly complex because of the thousands of choices of what can be measured and the variety of needs of the people that require and use the measures. A good overall performance measurement system is balanced, relevant, factual, and responsive to the users of the performance information. Most of all, the measures must drive performance toward the desired behavior. Most scholars and practitioners today advocate some form of "balanced scorecard" (See *Vital Signs*, Amacom 1993 by Steven Hronec, Arthur Andersen) so that measures of performance can be viewed from different perspectives, including from financial and operating perspectives, customers' and suppliers' perspectives, and product/service and innovations/creativity perspectives.

All of these perspectives on performance have value to the organization. In fact, they are dependent on one another. Without creative accounting, it is difficult to imagine situations where supplier quality and delivery performance are declining, products are late to market, and profits are increasing. Improving business process and activity performance would be useless if the products or services made by those activities did not meet customer requirements and needs—the most efficient producer of buggy whips is long gone. It is the relationship, dependency, and linkage of these perspectives that cause people to begin looking at an organization in a balanced way, much like the driver of an automobile who uses a panel of controls, measures, and indicators to reach an intended destination.

Measurement of activity performance is an important part of the organization's overall performance measure system. Improving the activities associated with creating, marketing, delivering, and supporting the organization is a fundamental driver to all viewpoints of performance. Yet, most organizations do not drive performance measurement to the activity level. Activities can be linked, integrated, and used to strengthen the existing performance measurement system of the organization. A good place to start is by linking activities to the top 10 to 12 current and important measures of overall organization performance. This can be accomplished with a simple matrix like that illustrated in Exhibit 11–1.

Exhibit 11–1.   Using ABM to Support Performance Measures

	Measure # 1	Measure # 2	Measure # 3	Measure N
Activity #1	●	●	●	◗
Activity # 2	◗	◗	O	O
Activity # 3	O	O	◗	O
Activity N	●	●	O	O

● High
◗ Medium
O Low

In Exhibit 11–1, the important and current measures of organization performance are shown across the top, with activities listed in the rows. Activities are linked to these measures by assigning a value that represents the importance of that activity to achieving the measurement. In the exhibit, each activity is linked to each measure on the basis of a high (darkened circle), medium (half-darkened circle), or low (open circle) correlation of the activity to the performance measure. Activities that are important to the top 10 to 12 measures of organizational performance are visual—the darker, the better. Also identified will be activities that have no or low impact on the important measures of organizational performance. By reading down the matrix, existing measures that are not adequately supported by activities are identified. This could also indicate that the current measurement system might be out of date or might be measuring things that are not important.

Integrating and linking activity-based measures of performance to the current and existing performance measurement system will strengthen it significantly. Activities are the common dominator and cornerstone of the horizontal organization. Measuring the performance of activities is an integral part of the organization's total performance measurement system and should be linked to other measures of performance so that relationships, dependencies, and synergies are understood.

IMPROVEMENT INITIATIVES

The value and benefit of ABM to the organization is created when the information results in better decisions, actions, and improvements. Therefore, the integration and linkage of ABM information to improvement initiatives, whether formal or informal, is vital. Activity-based management information systems report information on activities—the same activities that are the focal point of improvement initiatives. Activity-based management information must be integrated, linked, and used to support these initiatives.

The ABM system supports improvement initiatives by providing basic and fundamental activity information and data that people can use to measure the progress of improvement initiatives and to judge the result of effort. Using activity-based information and data to compare, or benchmark, activity performance is another way to support improvement initiatives and to establish improvement goals. Cost driver information supports improvement initiatives by linking improvement efforts to root cause.

Activity-based management information can be used to prioritize and select those improvement opportunities that have the highest probability of success. For example, activities can be scored against a set of criteria as basis for selection. The criteria could include total activity cost, potential for improvement (i.e., nonvalue added), contribution to strategy/goals of the organization, importance to customer, downstream cost driver, ability to influence cost drivers, and a people readiness factor. Criteria could be added, deleted, or weighted and are organization specific. The framework can be applied at the department level, at the branch level, to an individual plant or facility, or even to an entire company.

In terms of deploying this approach, again, a simple matrix works fine. List activities in rows with the criteria in columns across the top. Each activity is scored on the basis of 1 (low) to 5 (high) for each criterion. Guidelines for the assignment of scores for each criterion have been established and set forth in Exhibit 11–2.

Total activity cost is the first criterion. All organizations have high-cost and low-cost activities. High-cost activities are scored a five; low-cost activities are scored as one. The improvement potential criterion is a quantified estimate of the improvement opportunity. High potential for improvement is scored high, low potential is scored low. Much of the work done to support this estimate would have been completed by the value analysis performed as part of the ABM implementation. Another criterion is contribution to strategy or strategic objectives. Some activities are more important to the execution of strategy than others. Activities considered critical to the execution of strategy are scored high. Those activities that do not contribute to strategy or strategic goals are scored low.

Exhibit 11–2. Activity Scoring Guideline

	5	4	3	2	1
Total activity cost	High	Medium high	Medium	Medium low	Low
Improvement potential	25%	20 to 25%	10 to 19%	5 to 9%	Less than 5%
Importance to strategy/ strategic goals	Critical	Important	Necessary	Helpful	Does not contribute
Importance to customer	Very	Quite	Somewhat	Minimal	Not important
Downstream cost driver	Substantial impact	High impact	Moderate impact	Some impact	No impact
Ability to influence activity cost drivers	Easy short-term	Easy medium-term	Moderate short-term	Moderate long-term	Difficult to influence
People readiness	Drivers of change	Ready/willing to change	Willing	Skeptic	Resistant to change

Another criterion is the importance of the activity to the external customer. Activities important to the customer (i.e., bill customer) are scored high. Activities that are not important to the customer (i.e., pay vendors) are scored low. This is an important criterion to consider when selecting activities for improvement and can be weighted in the scoring to reflect its importance.

The impact of activity performance on downstream costs and the ability to influence the activity cost drivers can vary and are also important criteria to consider. Activities (i.e., design activities) that, if performed poorly, cause/drive cost in other activities downstream are scored high. Activities that do not impact other activities are scored low. Cost drivers that are easy to influence in the short term are scored high; those that cannot be influenced except over the very long term are scored low. The last criterion is a people readiness factor. People are associated with activities, and some are more ready for change than others. Those activities where the people are innovative, creative, and drivers of change would be scored high. Militants and resisters are scored low.

After the activities are scored, the matrix can be evaluated and activities selected for improvement. Do not just add up the scores and select the high score. In fact, do not even add up the scores. Study the matrix and use good business judgement to select activities for improvement. Look for two kinds of improvement efforts:

1. Efficiency. High-cost activities that are important to the customer, critical to meeting strategic goals, and drivers of downstream costs are activities the organization wants to improve. Select on the basis of potential for improvement and ability to influence cost drivers.

2. Effectiveness. Activities that are not important to the customer and make no contribution to strategic goals are activities to reduce/ eliminate. Select on the basis of total cost and potential for improvement.

Activity-based management information can be readily linked to organizations that use the cost of quality as part of their improvement initiatives. *Cost of quality* is defined as all the resources expended for appraisal costs, prevention costs, and both internal and external failure costs of activities and cost objects.

Accountants and financial people have always provided cost information about scrap, rework, disputed claims, warranty expenses, and similar costs in order to quantify the cost of internal failure. However, the information provided was limited, both in definition and in scope, and represented only the tip of the improvement iceberg. Cost of quality is intented to represent the total improvement iceberg. Activity-based management systems can be linked and integrated to the cost of quality because they accomplish the following:

1. Capture activities and related costs associated with appraisal, prevention, and internal failure costs.

2. Capture the cost of activities that do not add value but do not fail and, therefore, are not included in the cost of quality calculation (non-value-added activities).

3. Capture the activities and costs that are performed internally because of an external failure (i.e., activities associated with warranty repairs and returned shipments). Lost sales, missed opportunities, and damage of customer's goodwill are examples of external failure costs that are not captured or reported in most ABM systems.

Activity-based management information augments the cost of quality and provides credibility to the numbers because the information is tied to the basic financial records of the organization. The cost of quality numbers lose credibility in situations where the dollars of waste are declining, but there is no change in the overall cost structure or profits of the organization. Because ABM accounts for all costs, reported improvements, if not real, will show up somewhere else. It is not one or the other. Activity-based management and the cost of quality work together to provide an accurate reporting of improvement potential to managers.

CORE COMPETENCIES

Linkage and integration of ABM information should be driven to core competencies. Core competencies are important because they define the basis of competitive advantage. At least three tests can be applied to a core competency:

♦ A core competency provides potential access to a wide variety of markets.

♦ A core competency should make a significant contribution to the perceived customer benefits of the end product.

♦ A core competency should be difficult for competitors to imitate.

In reality, core competencies are not managed directly. To a large degree, it is those activities that created the core competency that are managed directly. Activity-based management provides information that can be used to strengthen core competencies by identifying those activities that are critical to the competency. Investment can be targeted to those activities. Focus can also be placed on those activities that have the greatest impact on fulfilling core competencies.

Linkage to core competencies could be established using a matrix and deployed in a manner similar to performance measurements. Activities remain in the rows and core competencies replace the performance measures in the column headings. Like the performance measures, activities can be linked to core competencies on the basis of high (darkened circle), medium (half-darkened circle), and low (open circle) correlation.

One final point. Continuous improvements are essential for sustaining and enhancing core competencies. The linkage and integration of ABM information with improvement initiatives provides a base structure to link core competencies.

COMPENSATION AND REWARD SYSTEMS

Activity-based management information, when integrated and linked to compensation, are pay-for-performance models of compensation and reward. Linkage and integration of ABM to the compensation and reward systems of the organization will drive full integration. People pay attention to those matters and measures that are visible, given attention by management, and that affect their paychecks. In many respects, compensation has always been linked and integrated with activities. Employees are paid for doing activities. Most job descriptions include description of activities and tasks. Organizations pay and hire people to do the activities required to deliver their products/services to the customer and to run and administer the business. Paychecks are compensation for doing organizational activities. Activities that require significant skill levels or specialized knowledge have always been compensated at higher levels than those activities that require minimal skill or knowledge.

Activity-based management information can be specifically integrated and linked with gain sharing programs. Gain sharing is different from profit sharing in that organizations share gains in performance, even if the profit levels are not satisfactory. Proponents of gain sharing note that there are many factors associated with the amount of profit an organization makes, and much of it cannot be controlled. By sharing performance gains, not profits, employees are incented to improve performance even if the reported profits are down. Paying for performance improvements when profits are down requires a high level of satisfaction that the gain is real. Activity-based management information can be linked and integrated to the gain sharing program and used as the basis for measuring the dollar savings of the improvement being shared.

VALUE-BASED MANAGEMENT

Professional managers have the obligation and responsibility to create value for the business owners who have entrusted them with capital investment. As a minimum, organizations must earn their cost of capital just to keep the owners whole. Anything less than that destroys value. Many organizations have embraced value-based management as the cornerstone for value creation. One acronym for value-based management is EVA™ (Economic Value Added), made popular by Stern Steward of New York. EVA is the difference, expressed in dollars, between the economic return on investment and the cost of capital for the business. It represents the amount of value created for shareholders, given the base return requirement associated with the business risk.

What makes value-based management so interesting is the linkage between what can be measured off the books and the factors that drive an increase in market price. The key drivers that increase value are improving margins, growing revenues, increasing asset utilization, and managing capital structure. Most of the key drivers are controllable and can be linked and integrated with the ABM information system.

Improving Margins
♦ Continuous improvement and re-engineering of business processes and activities.
♦ Increasing productivity and efficiency instead of cost cutting.
♦ Expanding revenues in high-margin products and services.

Growing Revenues
♦ Line extensions of new products and services that leverage existing investment.
♦ New business opportunities that create value.

♦ Prioritize business processes and activities that create value to the organization.

Increasing Asset Utilization

♦ Increasing turnover of working capital, especially receivables and payables.

♦ Increasing productivity of fixed assets through process improvement and re-engineering.

STRATEGIC AND OPERATIONS PLANNING

The purpose of a strategic plan is to identify long-term threats and opportunities, evaluate strategic alternatives, and then select the long-term strategy that will create the most value over the long term. Operating plans represent a more detailed set of objectives, actions, responsibilities, measures, resources, and priorities, to be executed in the short term. Activities represent the work necessary to accomplish all that has been set out to do in both the strategic and operation plans. Strategic plans, operating plans, and activities should be linked and integrated to one another.

Activities bridge the strategic and operation plans. Plans and strategies are implemented by properly identifying and directing those activities and actions necessary to accomplish the organization's short- and long-term goals. Strategic and operations planning is improved by specifically identifying those critical activities that must be performed (and at what level) to accomplish the plan result. By linking and integrating strategies and plans to activities, strategy is linked to the offices, factory floors, service centers, and support areas where the activities of the organization are performed. Activities link the boardroom to the shop floor.

TRAINING AND EDUCATION

Activity-based management is linked and integrated in the organization when people use the information. This can be a big hurdle because most people do not know how to use ABM information. Just like we train people to use traditional financial information, we must also train people in the use of activity-based information. Activity-based management training and education material is widely available and can be purchased "off-the-shelf" from many firms. Unfortunately, this generic training does not often meet the specific needs of the company. A more effective approach is to design and develop company training material, taught by competent instructors. This demonstrates commitment and makes it personal. Company-specific training material is more effective for the following reasons:

1. Examples and case studies can be based on the specific business.

2. The material can be designed to fit existing tools, techniques, and methods. This reinforces what's already done, and drives it further into the organization.

3. Design can fit the existing learning culture. Some people require fast-paced, big-picture training. Others require a slower, detailed method.

4. Training materials designed with company logos look and feel more personal.

5. Exercises that contribute to an existing work situation can be designed. Specific work products which are useful to the company can be developed as part of the training.

Activity-based management training will be required to build on the existing skills and knowledge base. Training is required to enable people to apply activity management skills in their specific work situation. While customized training can be more expensive than off-the-shelf material, it provides the best return on the training investment over the long term.

EXISTING INFORMATION SYSTEMS

Accounting, finance, and management information systems should be linked and integrated with the ABM system. Much of the linkage and integration is built into the ongoing ABM system as it is developed. By the time the ABM system is providing reports and information, interfaces and connections would have already been built to collect existing data already in finance, accounting, and other management systems. Most of the commercial software systems for sale today are designed to link with existing management information systems.

On an ongoing basis, efforts must continually be expended to integrate and link the ABM system to existing information systems. Efforts may be required to link ABM with budgeting systems and systems used to set standards. As the base operating systems change and improve over time, this provides opportunity to further link and integrate the ABM system. Technological changes will improve both the way we collect data and use information. The new systems and methods that will evolve from these advancements in technology will offer additional opportunities to link and integrate the ABM system to the existing information systems of the organization.

BEST PRACTICES

In mid 1994, the APQC's IBC, the leader in cooperative benchmarking, and CAM-I, recognized as the world's leading consortium in the field of activity costing and management practices, joined together to conduct a study of best practices in the area of ABC and ABM. The study and related survey represented the most comprehensive piece of work ever undertaken in the emerging area of ABM. The intent was to search for and identify best practices in the installation, application, and use of ABM systems. The study for which I served as the Project Director was completed in April 1995.

As part of this study an attempt was made to identify all known ABM implementations undertaken in North America. Over 750 of the 3,000+ organizations identified were invited to participate in a detailed survey designed to identify ABM best practices. The instructions with the survey stated that only those organizations that had achieved positive results from ABM efforts need complete and respond to the survey. One hundred sixty-six qualified responses were received.

Based on the survey responses, 40 companies were identified as best practice sites, of which 15 participated and hosted site visits. Criteria for selection of best practice sites was maturity of installation, scale of coverage, scope of application, results attained, and anticipated learning opportunities. The selection of site visits was based on availability, scheduling, and willingness to participate. The 15 site visits selected were representative of the 40 organizations identified as best practice.

While much of the study results and findings are proprietary to the organizations who sponsored and participated in the study, the ABM best practice model developed and published as a part of the study contains valuable nonproprietary information. This best practice model, shown in Exhibit 11–3, identified five areas of best practice summarized under the categories of methodology and technology, management needs and directions, appli-

Exhibit 11–3. ABM Best Practice Model

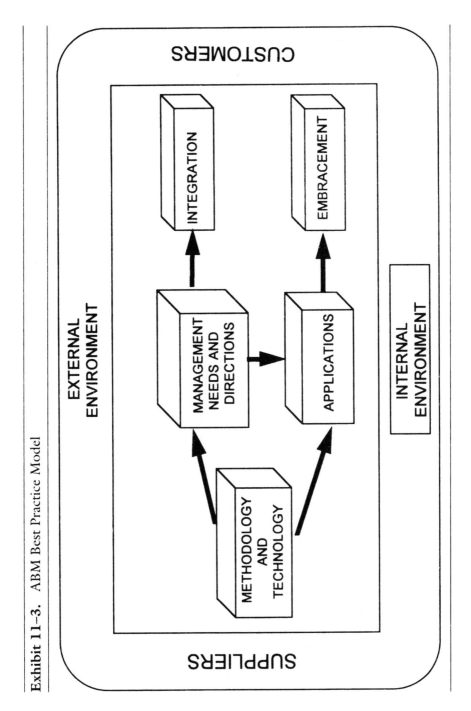

cations, integration, and embracement. Specific best practices were identified in each of these areas.

While not a best practice finding, it is interesting to note that almost all of the best practice companies initiated their ABM efforts as a response to external influences. Most often that external influence was caused by competitive pressure to reduce costs and improve profits. Innovation, technology, and regulatory environment were also cited as examples of external pressures.

Selected best practices from the best practice model are summarized below. The reader is challenged to use and consider ABM best practices in any ABM initiative that might be undertaken.

Best Practice companies manage their internal environment by nurturing a culture that supports change. Trust, team work, and team building were evident in all of the best practice companies that were visited. Each expressed a willingness to change. Missing from most best practice companies are hidden agendas.

Best Practice companies have a high degree of organizational acceptance that includes senior management involvement and commitment and strong linkage with other management initiatives. In general there is high delegation of authority with operating people requiring and using ABM information. Operating management is a partner with finance and has a focus on process orientation. Communication is open, honest, frequent, visible, and multifaceted.

Best Practice companies tend to be learning organizations that initiate extensive broad-based/multilevel training and cross-functional learning. Training beyond the traditional organizational structure, that is, supplier network is evident. At the ABM best practice sites the learning process is institutionalized rather than ad-hoc.

Best Practice companies use an ABM methodology that is consistent with current accepted practice. The companies use the two-stage cost-tracing methodology and consistent terms (CAM-I glossary). Systematic analysis of resource and activity drivers is undertaken and the diversity of drivers is balanced to business needs. Complexity of the ABM system is impacted by operations complexity, application breadth, intended uses, and detail level desired.

Best Practice companies use total cost in decision making and process improvement. Cost improvement initiatives are viewed in a holistic manner and exhibit a high level of customer-driven cost-consciousness. Costs are viewed in terms of value created and partnering concepts are used with both suppliers and customers.

Best Practice companies consistently seek new applications for using ABM information. While product costing is the dominant initial application, operational personnel prompt expansion into additional applications. At Best Practice sites, ABM is not a score keeping tool. Rather, it is used as a business analysis tool.

Best Practice companies address the entire value chain for their products. Suppliers are used to support product development and reductions in total part costs. Customers are used to support product development and reductions in customer support costs.

Best Practice companies use activity analysis to free capacity and grow revenue by realigning process flows in the plant to create capacity to add product and to use the capacity for the most profitable products. In addition, they value lost capacity in terms of manufacturing-related (nonproductive) and sales-related (idle capacity).

Best Practice companies achieve measurable process improvements by aggressively linking ABM information with improvement initiatives. Internal and external benchmarking and ABM data are used to drive and support improvement initiatives. Best Practice companies use ABM data to select areas for improvement.

Best Practice companies transfer ownership of ABM to line management. Activities and processes are defined by responsible managers, and relevant ABM data is made available to them to self-monitor their activities. Managers invent new uses of ABM information at Best Practice companies.

Best Practice companies develop ABM systems that are user-friendly and relatively easy to maintain. During development, users interrogate the system to ensure it can answer key operational and strategic questions. ABM systems are flexible enough to measure profitability by product, customer, or distribution channel. They avoid manually collecting new data; rather, they strive to use existing information.

Best Practice companies demonstrate a high degree of acceptance of ABM data by having a large number of people using the information. Activities and processes are defined and documented and ABM information is considered accurate, relevant, and easy to access and use. Users look for and demand the ABM data.

The CAM-I
Glossary of
Activity-Based
Management

Version 1.2

R-91-CMS-06

1250 E. COPELAND ROAD
SUITE 500
ARLINGTON, TX 76011

(817) 860-1654

Acknowledgments

Editors

Norm Raffish, Ernst & Young
Professor Peter B.B. Turney, Portland State University

Reviewers

Professor Robert Capettini, San Diego State University
Professor Donald K. Clancy, Texas Tech University
Professor Robin Cooper, Harvard Business School
Professor George Foster, Stanford University
Professor Don Madden, University of Kentucky
Professor James Reeve, University of Tennessee
James Brimson, Coopers & Lybrand, Deloitte
Barry J. Brinker, Journal of Cost Management
Tom Tessier, KPMG Peat Marwick

Sponsor and other Contributors

As with any mutual effort, there is no single individual responsible for this glossary's development. There were four CMS sponsor individuals who contributed to the definition of terms. They were Earl Reno of Douglas

Aircraft Co, Paolo Zanenga of CTE Consultenti Associati, Hidde van der Wal of Philips, and Norm Raffish of Ernst & Young. We also acknowledge the efforts of Chris Pieper, ABC Technologies, Inc.

In addition, we would like to thank the many CMS sponsors and our academic liaisons for reviewing the list of terms, contributing articles, and submitting various definitions that they found in use in their respective organizations.

Introduction

Objective

The primary objective of this glossary is to unify, standardize and where necessary, develop a set of terms pertaining to Activity-Based Management. It is hoped that this work will facilitate the understanding of Activity-Based Management and encourage better communication among those involved in the research, development, and implementation of this discipline.

Approach

This is the second glossary that the CAM-I CMS Program has produced. The first glossary was published in *Cost Management for Today's Advanced Manufacturing* in 1988. That glossary was a first attempt at defining the terms of the then emerging discipline known as Cost Management. The basis of that glossary was the design phase of the CMS Program begun in 1986 and was completed in early 1987.

This glossary has taken advantage of the experience gained in the intervening years of the CMS Program. We have had the benefit of significant additional research as well as several actual implementations of segments of Activity-Based Management. We should look at this glossary as the next step in the evolution of the research and development of this discipline.

In the Reference section of this Introduction, we acknowledge several sources, books, and articles of several authors who have helped both define and advance the theory and practice of Activity-Based Management.

Common Terminology

By the time this glossary was assembled, many competing terms were already in use. Given that several individuals and organizations were doing work in the area of Activity-Based Costing, it is not surprising to find identical terms with different meanings. It was one of the objectives of this project to compile a set of terms and definitions that would provide a single data base for the CAM-I CMS Program and others working in this area. We realize that this project in itself may add to the diversity of terms. However, it is essential that if the CAM-I CMS Program is to continue to develop and publish work on the theory and practice of Activity-Based Management, we need a single and accepted set of terms and definitions.

This issue became very clear when we looked at the variations of the term driver in use, as an example. It is the intent of this glossary to foster an industry standard for the terminology of this discipline. The work by others in this field should be fully recognized, acknowledged, and appreciated. While it is the intent of this glossary to fulfill the need of CAM-I sponsor members who require a common set of definitions that will permit them to communicate effectively with each other, in the longer view, an industry standard is far more preferable. If interested parties outside of CAM-I wish to adopt the terms and definitions contained in this work, we would consider that to be a positive comment on our work. We would also be glad to accept comment from outside of CAM-I on this work so that it can be continually improved as new editions are published.

Appendices

Contained in this glossary are several appendices. Due to the early stage of maturity and evolution of the Activity-Based Management, it was decided that several topics should be expanded in order to share our views on key issues. We hope that these additional sections assist in explaining why certain terms were chosen and the context in which we perceive their use.

Special Acknowledgment

The editors would like to extend a special acknowledgment to Michael Roberts, Program Manager, CAM-I CMS Program. Mike's role in this effort has been one of both as an individual reviewer and a project facilitator. Mike provided us with valuable insights, and coordinated our academic review effort. It is doubtful that we could have accomplished this project in the time allocated without his dedicated effort.

Glossary Committee

Norm Raffish, Chairman, Ernst & Young

Peter Turney, Portland State University

Mike Roberts, CAM-I

Tom Tessier, KPMG Peat Marwick

Glossary of Terms

ABC   see *activity-based costing*.

Absorption costing   A method of costing that assigns all or a portion of the manufacturing costs to products or other cost objects. The costs assigned include those that vary with the level of activity performed and also those that do not vary with the level of activity performed.

Activity   1. Work performed within an organization. 2. The aggregations of actions performed within an organization that are useful for purposes of activity-based costing.

Activity analysis   The identification and description of activities in an organization. Activity analysis involves determining what activities are done within a department, how many people perform the activities, how much time they spend performing the activities, what resources are required to perform the activities, what operational data best reflect the performance of the activities, and what value the activity has for the organization. Activity analysis is accomplished by means of interviews, questionnaires, observations, and reviews of physical records of work.

Activity attributes   Characteristics of individual activities. Attributes include cost drivers, cycle time, capacity, and performance measures. For example, a measure of the elapsed time required to complete an activity is an attribute. (See *cost driver* and *performance measures*.)

Activity capacity   The demonstrated or expected capacity of an activity under normal operating conditions, assuming a specified set of resources and over a long period of time. An example of this would be a rate of output for an activity expressed as 500 cycles per hour.

Activity cost assignment   The process in which the cost of activities are attached to cost objects using activity drivers. (See *cost object*, and *activity driver*.)

Activity cost pool   A grouping of all cost elements associated with an activity. (See *cost element*.)

Activity driver   A measure of the frequency and intensity of the demands placed on activities by cost objects. An activity driver is used to assign costs to cost objects. It represents a line-item on the bill of activities for a product or customer. An example is the number of part numbers, which is used to measure the consumption of material-related activities by each product, material type, or component. The number of customer orders measures the consumption of order-entry activities by each customer. Sometimes an activity driver is used as an indicator of the output of an activity, such as the number of purchase orders prepared by the purchasing activity. (See *intensity, cost object*, and *bill of activities*.)

Activity driver analysis   The identification and evaluation of the activity drivers used to trace the cost of activities to cost objects. Activity driver analysis may also involve selecting activity drivers with a potential for cost reduction. (See *Pareto analysis*.)

Activity level   A description of how an activity is used by a cost object or other activity. Some activity levels describe the cost object that uses the activity and the nature of this use. These levels include activities that are traceable to the product (i.e., unit-level, batch-level, and product-level costs), to the customer (customer-level costs), to a market (market-level costs), to a distribution channel (channel-level costs) and to a project, such as a research and development project (project-level costs).

Activity-based costing   A methodology that measures the cost and performance of activities, resources, and cost objects. Resources are assigned to activities, then activities are assigned to cost objects based on their use. Activity-based costing recognizes the causal relationships of cost drivers to activities.

Activity-based cost system   A system that maintains and processes financial and operating data on a firm's resources, activities, cost objects, cost drivers, and activity performance measures. It also assigns cost to activities and cost objects.

Activity-based management   A discipline that focuses on the management of activities as the route to improving the value received by the customer and the profit achieved by providing this value. This discipline includes cost driver analysis, activity analysis, and performance measurement. Activity-based management draws on Activity-based costing as its major source of information. (See *customer value*.)

Allocation   1. An apportionment or distribution. 2. A process of assigning cost to an activity or cost object when a direct measure does not exist. For example, assigning the cost of power to a machine activity by means of machine hours is an allocation, because machine hours is an indirect measure of power consumption. In some cases, allocations can be converted to tracing by incurring additional measurement costs. Instead of using machine hours to allocate power consumption, for example, a company can place a power meter on machines to measure actual power consumption. (See *tracing*.)

Assignment   See *cost assignment*.

Attributes   Characteristics of activities, such as cost drivers and performance measures. (See *cost driver* and *performance measure*.)

Attribution   See *tracing*.

Avoidable cost   A cost associated with an activity that would not be incurred if the activity was not required. The telephone cost associated with vendor support, for example, could be avoided if the activity were not performed.

Backflush costing   1. A costing method that applies costs based on the output of a process. The process uses a bill of material or a bill of activities explosion to draw quantities from inventory, through work-in-process, to finished goods; at any intermediate stage, using the output quantity as the basis.

These quantities are generally costed using standard costs. The process assumes that the bill of material (or bill of activities) and the standard costs at the time of backflushing represent the actual quantities and resources used in the manufacture of the product. This is important, since no shop orders are usually maintained to collect costs. 2. A costing method generally associated with repetitive manufacturing. (See *repetitive manufacturing* and *standard costing*.)

Benchmarking   See *best practices*.

Best practices   A methodology that identifies an activity as the benchmark by which a similar activity will be judged. This methodology is used to assist in identifying a process or technique that can increase the effectiveness or efficiency of an activity. The source may be internal (e.g., taken from another part of the company) or external (e.g., taken from a competitor.) Another term used is *competitive benchmarking.*

Bill of activities   A listing of the activities required (and, optionally, the associated costs of the resources consumed) by a product or other cost object.

Budget   1. A projected amount of cost or revenue for an activity or organizational unit covering a specific period of time. 2. Any plan for the coordination and control of resources and expenditures.

Capital decay   1. A quantification of the lost revenues or reduction in net cash flows sustained by an entity due to obsolete technology. 2. A measure of uncompetitiveness.

Carrying cost   See *holding cost.*

Competitive benchmarking   See *best practices.*

Continuous improvement program   A program to eliminate waste, reduce response time, simplify the design of both products and processes, and improve quality.

Cost Accounting Standards   1. Rules promulgated by the Cost Accounting Standards Board of the United States Government to ensure contractor compliance in the accounting of government contracts. 2. A set of rules issued by any of several authorized organizations or agencies, such as the American Institute of Certified Public Accountants (AICPA) or the Association of Chartered Accountants (ACA), dealing with the determination of costs to be allocated, inventoried, or expensed.

Cost assignment   The tracing or allocation of resources to activities or cost objects. (See *allocation* and *tracing.*)

Cost center   The basic unit of responsibility in an organization for which costs are accumulated.

Cost driver   Any factor that causes a change in the cost of an activity. For example, the quality of parts received by an activity (e.g., the percent that are defective) is a determining factor in the work required by that activity, because the quality of parts received affects the resources required to perform the activity. An activity may have multiple cost drivers associated with it.

Cost driver analysis   The examination, quantification, and explanation of the effects of cost drivers. Management often uses the results of cost driver analyses in continuous improvement programs to help reduce throughput time, improve quality, and reduce cost. (See *cost driver* and *continuous improvement program.*)

Cost element   An amount paid for a resource consumed by an activity and included in an activity cost pool. For example, power cost, engineering cost, and depreciation may be cost elements in the activity cost pool for a machine activity. (See *activity cost pool, bill of activities,* and *resource.*)

Cost object   Any customer, product, service, contract, project, or other work unit for which a separate cost measurement is desired.

Cost of quality   All the resources expended for appraisal costs, prevention costs, and both internal and external failure costs of activities and cost objects.

Cost pool   See *activity cost pool.*

Cross-subsidy   The improper assignment of costs among cost objects such that certain cost objects are overcosted while other cost objects are undercosted relative to the activity costs assigned. For example, traditional cost accounting systems tend to overcost high-volume products and undercost low-volume products.

Customer value   The difference between customer realization and sacrifice. *Realization* is what the customer receives, which includes product features, quality, and service. This takes into account the customer's cost to use, maintain, and dispose of the product or service. *Sacrifice* is what the customer gives up, which includes the amount the customer pays for the product plus time and effort spent acquiring the product and learning how to use it. Maximizing customer value means maximizing the difference between realization and sacrifice.

Differential cost   See *incremental cost.*

Direct cost   A cost that is traced directly to an activity or a cost object. For example, the material issued to a particular work order or the engineering time devoted to a specific product are direct costs to the work orders or products. (See *tracing.*)

Direct tracing   See *tracing*

Discounted cash flow   A technique used to evaluate the future cash flows generated by a capital investment. Discounted cash flow is computed by discounting cash flows to determine their present value.

Diversity   Conditions in which cost objects place different demands on activities or activities place different demands on resources. This situation arises, for example, when there is a difference in mix or volume of products that causes an uneven assignment of costs. Different types of diversity include: *batch-size, customer, market, product mix, distribution channel, and volume.*

Financial accounting   1. The accounting for assets, liabilities, equities, revenues, and expenses as a basis for reports to external parties. 2. A methodology that focuses on reporting financial information primarily for use by owners, external organizations, and financial institutions. This methodology is constrained by rule-making bodies such as the Financial Accounting Standards Board (FASB), the Securities Exchange Commission (SEC), and the American Institute of Certified Public Accountants (AICPA).

First-stage allocation   See *resource cost assignment.*

Fixed cost   A cost element of an activity that does not vary with changes in the volume of cost drivers or activity drivers. The depreciation of a machine, for example, may be direct to a particular activity, but it is fixed with respect to changes in the number of units of the activity driver. The designation of a cost element as fixed or variable may vary depending on the time frame of the decision in question and the extent to which the volume of production, activity drivers, or cost drivers changes.

Flexible factory   The objective of a flexible factory is to provide a wide range of services across many product lines in a timely manner. An example is a fabrication plant with several integrated manufacturing cells that can perform many functions for unrelated product lines with relatively short lead times.

Focused factory   The objective of a focused factory is to organize around a specific set of resources to provide low cost and high throughput over a narrow range of products.

Forcing   Allocating the costs of a sustaining activity to a cost object even though that cost object may not clearly consume or causally relate to that activity. Allocating a plant-level activity (such as heating) to product units using an activity driver such as direct labor hours, for example, forces the cost of this activity to the product. (See *sustaining activity.*)

Full absorption costing   See *absorption costing.*

Functional decomposition   Identifies the activities performed in the organization. It yields a hierarchical representation of the organization and shows the relationship between the different levels of the organization and its activities. For example, a hierarchy may start with the division and move down through the plant, function, process, activity, and task levels.

Holding cost   A financial technique that calculates the cost of retaining an asset (e.g., finished goods inventory or a building). Generally, the calculation includes a cost of capital in addition to other costs such as insurance, taxes, and space.

Homogeneity   A situation in which all the cost elements in an activity's cost pool are consumed in proportion to an activity driver by all cost objects. (See *cost element, activity cost pool,* and *activity driver.*)

Incremental cost   1. The cost associated with increasing the output of an activity or project above some base level. 2. The additional cost associated with selecting one economic or business alternative over another, such as the difference between working overtime or subcontracting the work. 3. The cost associated with increasing the quantity of a cost driver. (Also known as *differential cost.*)

Indirect cost   The cost that is allocated—as opposed to being traced—to an activity or a cost object. For example, the costs of supervision or heat may be allocated to an activity on the basis of direct labor hours. (See *allocation.*)

Intensity   The cost consumed by each unit of the activity driver. It is assumed that the intensity of each unit of the activity driver for a single activity is equal. Unequal intensity means that the activity should be broken into smaller activities or that a different activity driver should be chosen. (See *diversity.*)

Life Cycle   See *product life cycle.*

Net present value   A method that evaluates the difference between the present value of all cash inflows and outflows of an investment using a given rate of discount. If the discounted cash inflow exceeds the discounted outflow, the investment is considered economically feasible.

Non-value-added activity   An activity that is considered not to contribute to customer value or to the organization's needs. The designation non-value-added reflects a belief that the activity can be redesigned, reduced, or eliminated without reducing the quantity, responsiveness, or quality of the output required by the customer or the organization. (See *customer value* and *value analysis.*)

Obsolescence   A product or service that has lost its value to the customer due to changes in need or technology.

Opportunity cost   The economic value of a benefit that is sacrificed when an alternative course of action is selected.

Pareto analysis   The identification and interpretation of significant factors using Pareto's rule that 20 percent of a set of independent variables is responsible for 80 percent of the result. Pareto analysis can be used to identify cost drivers or activity drivers that are responsible for the majority of cost incurred by ranking the cost drivers in order of value. (See *cost driver analysis* and *activity driver analysis*.)

Performance measures   Indicators of the work performed and the results achieved in an activity, process, or organizational unit. Performance measures may be financial or nonfinancial. An example of a performance measure of an activity is the number of defective parts per million. An example of a performance measure of an organizational unit is return on sales.

Present value   The discounted value of a future sum or stream of cash flows.

Process   A series of activities that are linked to perform a specific objective. For example, the assembly of a television set or the paying of a bill or claim entails several linked activities.

Product family   A group of products or services that have a defined relationship because of physical and production similarities. (The term *product line* is used interchangeably.)

Product life cycle   The period that starts with the initial product specification and ends with the withdrawal of the product from the marketplace. A product life cycle is characterized by certain defined stages, including research, development, introduction, maturity, decline, and abandonment.

Product line   See *product family*.

Profit center   A segment of the business (e.g., a project, program, or business unit) that is accountable for both revenues and expenses.

Project   A planned undertaking, usually related to a specific activity, such as the research and development of a new product or the redesign of the layout of a plant.

Project costing   A cost system that collects information on activities and costs associated with a specific activity, project, or program.

Repetitive manufacturing   The manufacture of identical products (or a family of products) in a continuous flow.

Resource   An economic element that is applied or used in the performance of activities. Salaries and materials, for example, are resources used in the performance of activities. (See *cost element*.)

Resource cost assignment   The process by which cost is attached to activities. This process requires the assignment of cost from general ledger accounts to activities using resource drivers. For example, the chart of accounts may list information services at a plant level. It then becomes necessary to trace (assuming that tracing is practical) or to allocate (when tracing is not practical) the cost of information services to the activities that benefit from the information services by means of appropriate resource drivers. It may be necessary to set up intermediate activity cost pools to accumulate related costs from various resources before the assignment can be made. (See *activity cost pool* and *resource driver.*)

Resource driver   A measure of the quantity of resources consumed by an activity. An example of a resource driver is the percentage of total square feet of space occupied by an activity. This factor is used to allocate a portion of the cost of operating the facilities to the activity.

Responsibility accounting   An accounting method that focuses on identifying persons or organizational units that are accountable for the performance of revenue or expense plans.

Risk   The subjective assessment of the possible positive or negative consequences of a current or future action. In a business sense, risk is the premium asked or paid for engaging in an investment or venture. Often risk is incorporated into business decisions through such factors as hurdle rates or the interest premium paid over a prevailing base interest rate.

Second-stage allocation   See *activity cost assignment.*

Standard costing   A costing method that attaches costs to cost objects based on reasonable estimates or cost studies and by means of budgeted rates rather according to actual costs incurred.

Sunk costs   Costs that have been invested in assets for which there is little (if any) alternative or continued value except salvage. Using sunk costs as a basis for evaluating alternatives may lead to incorrect decisions. Examples are the invested cost in a scrapped part or the cost of an obsolete machine.

Support costs   Costs of activities not directly associated with production. Examples are the costs of process engineering and purchasing.

Surrogate activity driver   An activity driver that is not descriptive of an activity, but that is closely correlated to the performance of the activity. The use of a surrogate activity driver should reduce measurement costs without significantly increasing the costing bias. The number of production runs, for example, is not descriptive of the material disbursing activity, but the number of production runs may be used as an activity driver if material disbursements coincide with production runs.

Sustaining activity   An activity that benefits an organization at some level (e.g., the company as a whole or a division, plant, or department), but not any specific cost object. Examples of such activities are preparation of financial statements, plant management, and the support of community programs.

Target cost   A cost calculated by subtracting a desired profit margin from an estimated (or a market-based) price to arrive at a desired production, engineering, or marketing cost. The target cost may not be the initial production cost, but instead the cost that is expected to be achieved during the mature production stage. (See *target costing.*)

Target costing   A method used in the analysis of product and process design that involves estimating a target cost and designing the product to meet that cost. (See *target cost.*)

Technology costs   A category of cost associated with the development, acquisition, implementation, and maintenance of technology assets. It can include costs such as the depreciation of research equipment, tooling amortization, maintenance, and software development.

Technology valuation   A nontraditional approach to valuing technology acquisitions that may incorporate such elements as purchase price, start-up costs, current market value adjustments, and the risk premium of an acquisition.

Throughput   The rate of production of a defined process over a stated period of time. Rates may be expressed in terms of units of products, batches produced, dollar turnover, or other meaningful measurements.

Traceability   The ability to assign a cost by means of a causal relationship directly to an activity or a cost object in an economically feasible way. (See *tracing.*)

Tracing   The assignment of cost to an activity or a cost object using an observable measure of the consumption of resources by the activity or cost object. Tracing is generally preferred to allocation if the data exist or can be obtained at a reasonable cost. For example, if a company's cost accounting system captures the cost of supplies according to which activity uses the supplies, the costs may be traced—as opposed to allocated—to the appropriate activities. Tracing is also called *direct tracing.*

Unit cost   The cost associated with a single unit of the product, including direct costs, indirect costs, traced costs, and allocated costs.

Value-added activity   An activity that is judged to contribute to customer value or satisfy an organizational need. The attribute "value-added" reflects a belief that the activity cannot be eliminated without reducing the quantity, responsiveness, or quality of output required by a customer or organization. (See *customer value.*)

Value analysis   A cost reduction and process improvement tool that utilizes information collected about business processes and examines various attributes of the processes (e.g., diversity, capacity, and complexity) to identify candidates for improvement efforts. (See *activity attribute* and *cost driver.*)

Value chain   The set of activities required to design, procure, produce, market, distribute, and service a product or service.

Value-chain costing   An activity-based cost model that contains all activities in the value chain.

Variance   The difference between an expected and actual result.

Variable cost   A cost element of an activity that varies with changes in volume of cost drivers and activity drivers. The cost of material handling to an activity, for example, varies according to the number of material deliveries and pickups to and from that activity. (See *cost element, fixed cost,* and *activity driver.*)

Waste   Resources consumed by unessential or inefficient activities.

Willie Sutton rule   Focus on the high-cost activities. The rule is named after bank robber Willie Sutton, who—when asked "why do you rob banks?"—is reputed to have replied "because that's where the money is."

Work cell   A physical or logical grouping of resources that performs a defined job or task. The work cell may contain more than one activity. For example, all the tasks associated with the final assembly of a product may be grouped in a work cell.

Work center   A physical area of the plant or factory. It consists of one or more resources where a particular product or process is accomplished.

APPENDIX A

Choice of Terms

Driver

There is probably no term, other than activity, that has become more identified with Activity-Based Costing as the term driver and its several variations. The problem is that it has been applied to several entities with varying meanings. It is often difficult to understand whether the use of the term driver is related to a causal effect (cost or input driver) or to the output of an activity (cost or output driver). In addition, terms such as first and second stage driver have come into use which also describe entities similar to resource and activity driver.

In this glossary we have chosen to use the term cost driver as the causal event that influences the quantity of work, and therefore costs, in an activity. We believe that by restricting the definition of cost driver to one meaning, it will facilitate its understanding.

We also appended the term driver to two other entities. The first deals with the mechanism of assigning resources to activities. That we call a resource driver. The second deals with the mechanism of assigning activity costs to cost objects. That we call an activity driver.

We hope that by limiting the use of the word driver to three clearly defined entities, we can prevent misinterpretation or misuse of the term.

Non-Value-Added and Sustaining Activities

There are many activities in an organization that do not contribute to customer value, responsiveness, and quality. That does not mean that those activities can be eliminated or even reduced without doing harm to the business entity. Preparing required regulatory reports certainly does not add to the value of any cost object or to the satisfaction of the customer. However, that activity does have value to the organization since it permits it to function in a legal manner. The business community needs to distinguish between activities that are:

not required at all and can be eliminated, (e.g., a duplication of effort),

ineffectively accomplished and can be reduced or redesigned (e.g., due to outdated policies or procedures), or

required to sustain the organization and therefore may not be able to be reduced or eliminated (e.g., provide plant security).

Diversity

In the definition of this term we listed several examples of types of diversity that could influence cost assignment. We did not attempt to define all the possible types of diversity, or to give examples of each. However, we feel that a good understanding of the issues surrounding diversity is important to insure that the process of cost assignment is equitable and accurate among cost objects. We would refer the reader to an article published in the *Harvard Business Review* (Sept–Oct 1988), by Robert Kaplan and Robin Cooper entitled, "Measuring Costs Right: Make the Right Decisions" which covers many of the aspects of this topic.

APPENDIX B

Illustrations

The CAM-I ABC Basic Model

Exhibit B–1, the first illustration of the basic model, is an attempt to establish a generic illustration that can be used to assist in explaining the concepts of Activity-Based Costing. The model should be thought of as a template that can be adapted for various purposes. The model should not be thought of as a flow chart of activity-based costing. It is meant to be a conceptual diagram that allows the reader to gain a high level understanding of the ABC processes.

There are two axes to the model. The vertical one deals with the classic two-stage cost assignment view. In the expanded model, their are three entities and two processes. The resource entity contains all available means upon which the selected activity can draw. The resource cost assignment process contains the structure and tools to trace and allocate costs to the activity. It is during this process that the applicable resource drivers are developed as the mechanism to convey resource costs to the activity. The activity entity is where work is performed. In this view, the activity is part of the cost structure. It is where resources are converted to some type of output. The activity cost assignment process contains the structure and tools to assign costs to cost objects, utilizing activity drivers as the mechanism to accomplish this assignment.

This cost assignment view is basically a "snap-shot" view in the sense that the Balance Sheet on a financial statement is only a view of the business at the moment the accounts were tallied. In this sense, the cost as-

Exhibit B–1. The CAM-I ABC Basic Model

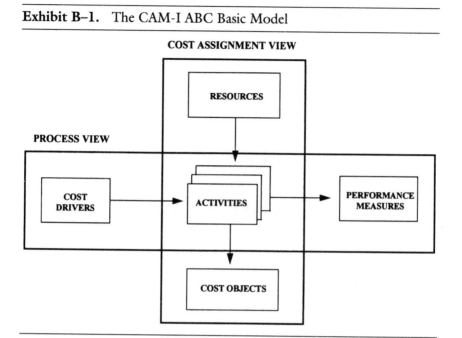

signment view can be seen as the structure and rules by which cost assignment takes place at some specific time. This time period may be at the end of a month, quarter, or any other time period which may or may not coincide with an accounting reporting period.

The horizontal axis contains the process view. This is a dynamic view, similar to the Income and Expense statement that reports on what has/is happening. This part of the process is initiated by a causal occurrence we call a cost driver. The cost driver is the agent that causes the activity to utilize resources to accomplish some designated work. In this view the activity is some type of active work center. During and after the activity work effort, performance data are collected. The performance measure of activities entity houses the evaluative criteria by which the organization can determine the efficiency and effectiveness of the activities work effort. It should be noted that there are many other performance measures, such as market share and return on equity, that are not included in the performance measures included in the ABC model.

The process view will constantly be changing. Each time a cost driver initiates work in an activity, new results will be obtained. It is therefore critical that applicable and realistic performance measures be established so that tracking of activity results can be monitored and improved on a continuing basis. ABC, through its reporting and analysis, can become an enabler of other process changes such as synchronous manufacturing, Design for Manufacturing, and Design for Assembly.

Expanded Process View

Exhibit B–2 is a more realistic view of what really takes place in an organization. There are many processes in progress, and each is usually made up of several linked activities. The illustration points out that the output (cost object) of any activity, may be the input (cost driver) of the next activity. This relationship, of several activities forming a process or subprocess, offers the opportunity to link congruent performance measurements which would offer a more appropriate view of the effectiveness and efficiency of that process.

CAM-I Expanded ABC Model

Exhibit B–3 displays an expanded view of the ABC model. Depicted in this illustration are the resource cost assignment and activity cost assignment processes, and their respective data bases of drivers. Another addi-

---

Exhibit B–2.   Expanded Process View

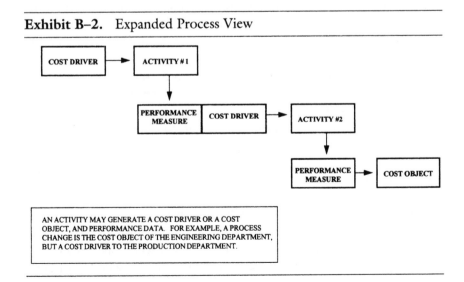

Exhibit B–3.   CAM-I Expanded ABC Model

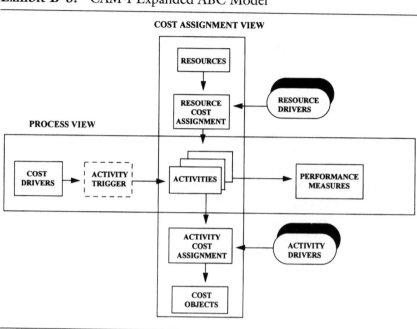

tion is an entity called the activity trigger. This term is not defined in the glossary as it pertains to an activity-based costing system rather than to the ABC methodology. The activity trigger is often, but not always, the link between the occurrence of a cost driver and the initiation of action in an activity. As an example, the mere occurrence of scrap does not in itself initiate an activity. There will need to be some management authorization to proceed before a replacement part is produced. In an information system about ABC, the activity trigger will often be the collection point for the information about the cost driver. The other entities depicted are cost drivers, activities, cost objects, and activity related performance measures.

ABC Model Example

Included as well in this section is Exhibit B–4 that displays how the model might be applied to a functional activity. The activity illustrated here is the purchasing activity at a department level. The particular task involved is generating purchase orders. One can see by the metrics selected for per-

Exhibit B–4. ABC Model Example

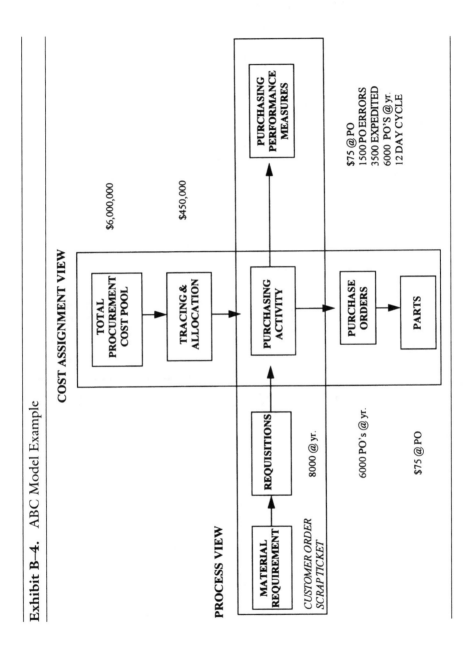

COST ASSIGNMENT VIEW

PROCESS VIEW

TOTAL PROCUREMENT COST POOL

TRACING & ALLOCATION

PURCHASING ACTIVITY

PURCHASE ORDERS

PARTS

PURCHASING PERFORMANCE MEASURES

$6,000,000

$450,000

$75 @ PO
1500 PO ERRORS
3500 EXPEDITED
6000 PO'S @ yr.
12 DAY CYCLE

MATERIAL REQUIREMENT

REQUISITIONS

CUSTOMER ORDER
SCRAP TICKET

8000 @ yr.

6000 PO's @ yr.

$75 @ PO

formance measures, that a trend analysis could certainly identify candidate tasks for a continuous improvement program.

Activity-Based Management Model

Exhibit B–5 is a view of Activity-Based Management. It depicts the key relationship between ABC, and the management analysis tools that are needed to bring full realization of the benefits of ABC to the organization. ABC is a methodology that can yield significant information about cost drivers, activities, resources, and performance measures. However, ABM is a discipline that offers the organization the opportunity to improve the value of its products and services.

Exhibit B–5.   Activity-Based Management Model

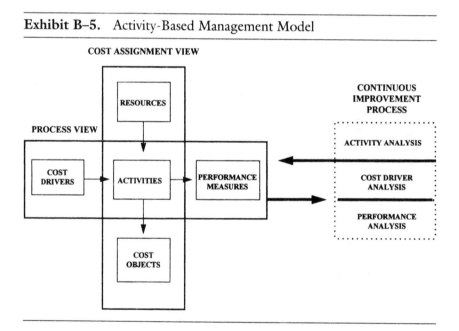

APPENDIX C

References

In attempting to use as much of what was available in terms of definitions, there were several reference documents that provided excellent source material. They are:

1. *A Dictionary for Accountants* by Eric L. Kohler, Fifth Edition (Englewood Cliffs: Prentice-Hall, 1975)
2. "Management Accounting Terminology, Statement on Management Accounting Number 2A" (National Association of Accountants, May 1990)
3. *Webster's Ninth New Collegiate Dictionary,* (Merriam-Webster, Inc., 1984)
4. *Cost Management for Today's Advanced Manufacturing,* Edited by C. Berliner and J.A. Brimson (Harvard Business School Press, 1988)

Activity-Based Costing has gained a significant measure of development and publicity in the past few years. Several individuals have made significant contributions to this growing body of knowledge. Through their articles, books, and lectures, they have influenced almost all of us who have worked in the field of Activity-Based Management. It is also fair to say that their efforts have influenced the content of this glossary.

1. H. Thomas Johnson and Robert S. Kaplan, *Relevance Lost: The Rise and Fall of Management Accounting*, (Harvard Business Review, 1987)

2. Thomas Johnson, a series of articles:

   Activity Management: Reviewing the Past and Future of Cost Management, (*Journal of Cost Management*, Winter 1990)

   Pitfalls in Using ABC Cost-Driver Information to Manage Operating Cost, (*Corporate Controller*, Jan/Feb 1991, coauthors T.P. Vance and R.S. Player)

   Activity Management: Past, Present, and Future, (*The Engineering Economist*, Spring 1991)

3. Robin Cooper, a series of articles:

   Schrader Bellows, (*Harvard Business School* Case, 1986)

   The Rise of Activity Based Costing, in four parts (*Journal of Cost Management*, Summer and Fall 1988, Winter 1989 and Spring 1990)

   The Two Stage Procedure in Cost Accounting, in two parts (*Journal of Cost Management*, Spring and Summer 1987)

   Cost Classifications in Unit-Based and Activity-Based Management Cost Systems, (*Journal of Cost Management*, Fall 1990)

4. Robert S. Kaplan, Union Pacific, (*Harvard Business School* Case, 1987)

5. Robert S. Kaplan, One Cost System Isn't Enough. (*Harvard Business Review*, J-F 1988)

6. Robin Cooper and Robert S. Kaplan, Measure Costs Right: Make the Right Decisions. (*Harvard Business Review*, S-O 1988)

7. Peter B.B. Turney, a series of articles:

   What is the Scope of Activity-Based Costing (*Journal of Cost Management*, Fall 1988)

   Ten Myths About Implementing Activity-Based Cost Systems (*Journal of Cost Management*, Spring 1990)

   The Impact of Continuous Improvement on the Design of Activity-Based Cost Systems, with James Reeve (*Journal of Cost Management*, Summer 1990)

How Activity-Based Costing Helps Reduce Cost (*Journal of Cost Management*, Winter 1991)

8. James Brimson, *Activity Accounting: An Activity-Based Cost Approach* (Coopers and Lybrand, John Wiley & Sons. 1991)

9. M. Stahl and G. Bound, editors, *Competing Globally Through Customer Value: The Management of Suprasystems.* (Greenwood Press, 1991)

10. Charles T. Horngren and George Foster, *Cost Accounting, A Managerial Emphasis* (Prentice-Hall, Inc. 1991)

11. Peter B. B. Turney, from a forthcoming book, *Common Cents: The ABC Performance Breakthrough* (Cost Technology, 1991)

Index

ABCM. *See* Activity-based
management (ABM)
ABC model (CAM-I)
basic, 231–33
example of, 234–36
expanded, 233–34
ABCost Manager, 188
ABC Technologies, Inc., 45, 49–50,
184
ABM. *See* Activity-based
management
Absorption costing, 217
Accuracy (in data), 179–80, 207
Acquisition analysis, 24
ACTIVA, 187
Activity, 71–72, 217
as basis for ABC, 2–5
costing, 51–53
criteria for selection of, 85–87
Activity analysis, 39–40, 69–71, 207,
217
bottom-up approach, 73, 85
measurement of value, 92–93
methods of, 72–73

top-down approach, 72, 73–85
Activity attribute, 74–75, 97, 217. *See
also* Capacity; Cost driver;
Performance measurement
Activity-based costing (ABC), vii–viii,
1, 5–7, 218
application example, 57–64
history of, 10–13
traditional costing compared to,
64–67
Activity-based cost management
(ABCM). *See* Activity-based
management (ABM)
Activity-based cost system, 218
Activity-based management (ABM), 1,
166, 193–94, 218–19
applications, 15–25
history of, 10–13
model of, 236
performance measurement in,
7–8
See also Customer value;
Information systems (ABM)
Activity-based tracing, 11

240

About the Nam

The National Association of Manufacturers (NAM) is the nation's oldest and largest broad-based industrial trade association. Its more than 13,000 member companies and subsidiaries, including 9,000 small manufacturers, are located in every state and produce approximately 85 percent of U.S. manufactured goods. Through its member companies and affiliated associations, the NAM represents every industrial sector, 185,000 businesses, and more than 18 million employees.

The NAM's mission is to enhance the competitiveness of manufacturers by shaping a legislative and regulatory environment conducive to U.S. economic growth in a global economy, and to increase understanding among policymakers, the media, and the general public about the importance of manufacturing to America's economic strength and standard of living.

The NAM is headquartered in Washington, D.C., and has regional offices across the nation. For more information on the NAM, call 202-637-3000.